LET'S GO, BRANDON!

VOL. 1

The Faux Pas, Fiascos, and Failures of the Biden-Harris Administration

BY BRANDON VALLORANI

FOREWORD BY JOE VISCONTI

Author Brandon Vallorani
Research Assistant Lita Sanders
Editor Liz Martin
Proofreader Jan Vallorani
Designer Brandon Vallorani

Printed in the United States of America

© 2022 Tolle Lege Press
TolleLegePress.com
A Division of Bravera Holdings, LLC
3330 Cobb Pkwy. Ste. #324-346
Acworth, GA 30101

ISBN: 979-8-9857901-9-1

DEDICATION

This book is dedicated to Bethany, Adam, Josiah, Isaac, Charity, Sarah, Levi, Oliver, Vivian, Theodore, and Dean. It is now upon you to carry the flame of liberty and pass our faith on to the next generation.

ENDORSEMENTS

"Congratulations to Brandon Vallorani for having the conviction, courage, and brilliance to step into the American Political Arena in the struggle to restore and enforce The Constitution of the United States of America!"
— Joe Visconti, Emmy Award-Winning Producer, Political Activist (20 years), Former West Hartford Connecticut Republican Town Councilor (2007-2009), Candidate for Connecticut Governor (2014), and Commentator

"This is a must-read for Americans who want Republicans to take back the White House in 2024. Going day by day through Biden's first year in office, Brandon calls the Biden-Harris Administration to account for their destructive policies and tyrannical executive orders. He doesn't stop there, however. He also provides hope with the conservative solution!"
— Mark Schaftlein, CEO of Conservative Broadcast Media & Journalism (OTC:CBMJ) and Host of The Schaftlein Report

"In his hard-hitting book, Brandon Vallorani chronicles the pathetic performance of the Biden regime's first year in power. He also exposes the tyranny lurking behind every executive order from this puppet President."
— Steven Hotze, M.D., Founder, Hotze Health & Wellness Center, Founder, Conservative Republicans of Texas

"Joe Biden has been a tornadic, F5, presidential disaster to our great nation. He's a joke of a president. A veritable *qualem muleirculam*. How anyone can still support this half-dead, carrier pigeon of Marxists' ideals is beyond me. Brandon Vallorani's new book, *Let's Go, Brandon!*, righteously jackhammers number forty-six into oblivion. Vallorani's fresh spicy tome should be air-dropped on every university campus. Thank you Brandon for writing this fire breathing expose of a man who's full of more crap than a collicky baby's diaper."

– Doug Giles, Artist & Best Selling Author

"Who better than Brandon Vallorani to reveal the drivers that gave birth to "Let's Go, Brandon!" This book adeptly catalogues Biden's daily screw-ups, Anti-America actions, and outright lies. You will gain clarity as to why "Let's Go, Brandon!" gave voice to the frustration and anger Patriots across America share against the deceptive, destructive Globalist "Great Reset" Agenda that Biden and his leftist tyrant crones are trying to cram down our throats. Hang in there while Brandon Vallorani articulates Hope. Hope to act as citizens to preserve our Liberty and Hope in the Creator God our Founding Fathers trusted in as the foundation of our Declaration of Independence and our Liberty."

– Gregory Blume, Managing Partner of Stone Meadow Homes & Director of Liberty Center for God & Country

TABLE OF CONTENTS

FOREWORD

The fictional election of Joe Biden assisted by 2,000 illegal Swing State Ballot Harvesting Mules amongst other outrageous election frauds transported America from the best of times to the worst of times.

The battle cry under President Trump was America First, which became quashed in 2020 during the Bio Terror attack from China, aka Covid-19. We were subsequently led backwards to harken Joe Biden's Battle Cry: America Last.

Many may wonder why the phrase "Let's Go, Brandon!" has become so popular, especially with its vulgar connotation. The answer to those wondering is that it proclaims with monumental passion and the most complex simplicity everything our founding fathers were saying to the British when they had had enough of British brutality, tyranny and lies. F--k King George.

When America has had enough of losing, watching their leaders lose on purpose, clearly throwing the game: they get angry. They got angry, they are angry, and they are demanding singular political standards, real ethics in government, common sense, affordable policies, the re-establishment of an objective news media, a non-surveillance state, fiscal discipline, a return to energy independence, secure borders, individual Liberty, equal Justice, and their God-given rights back.

Let's Go, Brandon!, with its timely insights and God-centered passion for truth will join in with other powerful voices to help all American Patriots endure the current state of clear, outrageous, and abject political treason we are experiencing under President Biden.

Congratulations to Brandon Vallorani for having the conviction, courage, and brilliance to step into the American Political Arena in the struggle to restore and enforce The Constitution of the United States of America!

– Joe Visconti
Emmy Award-Winning Producer, Political Activist (20 years), Former West Hartford Connecticut Republican Town Councilor (2007-2009), Candidate for Connecticut Governor (2014), and Commentator

President Donald J. Trump and Joe Visconti

INTRODUCTION

What does "Let's Go, Brandon!" really mean?

By now you've probably seen several "Let's Go, Brandon!" memes and products on social media. Brandon happens to be my name, so this trend really got my attention. Why so much excitement about a guy named Brandon?

Brandon Brown is the NASCAR driver who won his first Xfinity Series race at Talladega on October 2, 2021. Did the whole country become NASCAR fans overnight? As much as I love NASCAR, that is not the case. The phrase "Let's Go, Brandon," of course, refers to the viral video where the crowd is actually chanting "F--k Joe Biden" during Brandon's victory interview with NBC sports reporter, Kelli Stavast.

In what many believe to be a form of damage control, Kelli claimed the chant was actually "Let's Go, Brandon!" Perhaps she really didn't hear it correctly, but it's fairly obvious what is being said when you watch the interview on YouTube![1]

Either way, America didn't buy it. There's only so much the mainstream media can do to prop up and protect Joe Biden. As a result, "Let's Go, Brandon!" has become synonymous with "F--k Joe Biden."

---

1. https://youtu.be/axcmVFtwSM4

For months now, multiple sporting events have garnered large crowds chanting "F--k Joe Biden" in protest of the numerous gaffes and missteps he's been responsible for since he claimed office in January 2021.

FJB protests have exploded around the world. This should come as no surprise as his approval rating is somewhere between the sub-levels of the same basement where they've been illegally detaining pro-Trump supporters since January. Independents and even many Democrats are having serious buyer's remorse.

Americans are disgusted at the way he handled the withdrawal from Afghanistan, terrified over his lack of concern about our southern border, frustrated with high gas prices, struggling to stay afloat in a ruined economy, angered that he wants to coerce Americans to get a medical experiment against their will, and can't believe how many are still being paid to stay home instead of filling one of the millions of jobs available.

The list goes on and on. America is being destroyed while he fumbles over his teleprompter and sets up speeches from a staged White House scene! Are we in the movies? Please end the horror show now!

As a Christian and Patriot, I face a dilemma. Is it consistent with my Christian faith to tell the acting President of the United States to "F--k off?" No matter how wicked or vile our leaders may be, St. Paul the Apostle tells us how to respond in 1 Timothy 2:1-3 (NIV),

> "I urge, then, first of all, that petitions, prayers, intercession and thanksgiving be made for all people— for kings and all those in authority, that we may live peaceful and quiet lives in all godliness and holiness. This is good, and pleases God our Savior,"

And then there's his instruction in Romans 13: 1-7 (NIV),

> "Let everyone be subject to the governing authorities, for there is no authority except that which God has established. The authorities that exist have been established by God. Consequently, whoever rebels against the authority is rebelling against what God has instituted, and those who do so will bring judgment on themselves. For rulers hold no terror for those who do right, but for those who do wrong. Do you want to be free from fear of the one in authority? Then do what is right and you will be commended. For the one in authority is God's servant for your good. But if you do wrong, be afraid, for rulers do not bear the sword for no reason. They are God's servants, agents of wrath to bring punishment on the wrongdoer. Therefore, it is necessary to submit to the authorities, not only because of possible punishment but also as a matter of conscience. This is also why you pay taxes, for the authorities are God's servants, who give their full time to governing. Give to everyone what you owe them: If you owe taxes, pay taxes; if revenue,

then revenue; if respect, then respect; if honor, then honor."

Does this mean that we are supposed to turn a blind eye to leaders like Biden and their actions? No. The Prophets held Old Testament Kings accountable. In the New Testament, John the Baptist held King Herod accountable for his sins. Jesus held the religious leaders of his day accountable for their unbelief and hypocrisy. The Apostle Paul claimed his Roman citizenship when he was wrongly held without trial. It is the place of the Church, led by King Jesus, to hold the State to the standard of God's Law. The Bible is clear that all governments answer to Jesus Christ.

The prophet Isaiah foretold this would happen in Isaiah 9:6 (NIV),

> "For to us a child is born, to us a son is given, and the government will be on his shoulders. And he will be called Wonderful Counselor, Mighty God, Everlasting Father, Prince of Peace."

This was fulfilled after Jesus's resurrection and ascension. St. Paul says in 1 Corinthians 15: 23-24 (NIV),

> "Then the end will come, when he hands over the kingdom to God the Father after he has destroyed all dominion, authority and power. For he must reign until he has put all his enemies under his feet."

From the great Pharaohs and the Caesars to Alexander the Great and the Democrats of 2021, all either have or will answer to King Jesus. Ultimately, as a Christian, I believe only Jesus can curse the President of the United States. It is not *my* place.

As a Patriot, however, I stand with all Americans and their constitutional right to free speech. The highest law in the land says we have the right –– and dare I say the duty –– to criticize and hold our leaders accountable.

When President Trump was in office, the Left just came right out and said "F--k Trump" with no creativity whatsoever. At least conservatives have a G-rated euphemism, "Let's Go, Brandon!," which is far less offensive, but gets the point across!

The bottom line is this: I decided to write this book to validate your frustration with the disaster that currently occupies the White House. The truth will set us free. We must speak up to be heard over the mainstream media, Big Tech, woke mega-businesses, leftist campuses, Hollywood elites, etc.

With the help of my research assistant Lita Sanders, we've put together 12 chapters (one for each month of 2021) of the faux pas, fiascos, and failures of the Biden-Harris Regime in 2021. Many thanks to Liz Martin for her additional research and extensive editing of the following manuscript, and Jan Vallorani for her proof-reading skills.

If we unite and turn out to vote, we have a chance to win back Congress in 2022. And that is just one step away from ending the insanity and winning back the White House in 2024.

We can't stop there, however. While winning elections are important, they are not the ultimate solution. In the Epilogue, I challenge our modern pessimistic thinking with a long-term view of victory. I trust you will read it with an open mind and be encouraged that God wins in the end and we get to be a part of the process.

For the sake of our children and our grandchildren for whom this book is dedicated, we must prevail. Let's Go, Brandon!

For God & Country,

Brandon R. Vallorani

Brandon & Jan Vallorani with cousins Lisa & Chris Desko

PROLOGUE:
"RUN, JOE, RUN!"

Joseph Robinette Biden, Jr.'s 2020 Presidential campaign was his third attempt to be elected as Commander in Chief of the United States of America. His 1988 attempt was thwarted when he was discovered to have plagiarized during law school and in speeches, and he subsequently withdrew. He tried again in 2008 but Barack Obama was chosen as the Democratic candidate, with Joe Biden as his running mate.

Biden has long been known for gaffes and misspeaking, and his most recent campaign was no different. He accidentally announced his candidacy on March 17, 2019 at a dinner in Dover, Delaware.[2]

While he received an enthusiastic reception at that event, some writers wasted no time pointing out that while a second Trump term would be every liberal's nightmare, Biden had a history of "problematic" behavior. As liberal media outlet Vox summarized: "Joe Biden does slightly inappropriate stuff all the time."[3]

2.   Peter Wade, Biden Accidentally Says He's Running, Crowd Chants 'Run, Joe, Run!', *Rolling Stone*, March 17, 2019 https://www.rollingstone.com/politics/politics-news/biden-accidentally-announces-Presidential-run-809280/
3.   Matthew Yglesias, The controversy over Joe Biden's treatment of women, explained, Vox.com, April 3, 2019 https://www.vox.com/2019/4/2/18290345/joe-biden-lucy-flores-amy-lappos

Only a few years earlier, the Washington Post asked plaintively, "What are we going to do about Creepy Uncle Joe Biden?"[4] Photo galleries and video compilations abounded of the many times Biden got too close to women and even young girls, sniffing hair and whispering creepily in their ears.

Actress Rose McGowan claimed that her social media accounts were deactivated and shadow banned when she publicly criticized Joe Biden, accusing the Democratic party of working behind the scenes to censor her.[5]

Biden's performance in the early primaries was less than promising, as he came in fourth in the Iowa caucuses and fifth in the New Hampshire primary. However, after several contenders dropped out of the race and endorsed Biden — seen by many as an attempt to stop Bernie Sanders' nomination — Biden became the Democratic party's nominee.

In the second Presidential debate, President Trump accused Biden "of a pay-for-play scheme in Ukraine and China related to his son's business dealings in those two

---

4.   Alexandra Petri, What are we going to do about Creepy Uncle Joe Biden?, *The Washington Post*, February 18, 2015 https://www.washingtonpost.com/blogs/compost/wp/2015/02/18/what-are-we-going-to-do-about-creepy-uncle-joe-biden/
5.   David Ng, Rose McGowan says Facebook deactivated her account over Presidential debate, Breitbart, October 23, 2020.

countries."[6] Many Democrats took to a shoulder-shrugging position of "not my first choice, but...."

COVID-19 impacted the way in which people voted; early and mail-in voting became very popular options, despite concerns about the potential for voter fraud.

Ann Coulter put it: "They cheated the way they always do, by manufacturing votes for people they knew were not going to vote because they are dead, ineligible or apathetic. ...Presumably Democrats didn't abandon their usual vote-stealing methods, such as driving homeless people to the polls in exchange for a box lunch, "helping" nursing home residents fill out ballots, and waiting for the polls to close to discover pallets of uncounted ballots. This year, Democrats could also vote the millions of mail-in ballots littering the countryside."[7]

Donald Trump received 12 million more votes than he did in the 2016 election: 74,222,958 votes. That would be an all-time record for any Presidential candidate, had Joe Biden not been attributed with 81,283,098 votes.

6.   Edwin Mora, Breitbart Land: Data shows number one online story in America about debate is Biden corruption, October 24, 2020, https://www.breitbart.com/politics/2020/10/24/breitbart-land-data-shows-number-one-online-story-in-america-about-debate-is-biden-corruption/.
7.   Ann Coulter, Yes, they cheat. We have to win Georgia anyway, December 2, 2020 https://anncoulter.com/2020/12/02/yes-they-cheat-we-have-to-win-georgia-anywayx

Republicans were quick to point out what seemed to be evidence of clear-cut fraud to tip the scales in Joe Biden's favor, particularly as reporting indicators seemed skewed in favor of Biden.

Biden himself said on the day before Election Day, "We have put together, I think, the most extensive and inclusive voter fraud organization in the history of American politics."[8] Was he actually admitting that he was elected by fraudulent votes?

The Dominion electronic voting machines, used by at least 24 states in the 2020 election, were criticized long before, even by the Democrats. In 2019 they claimed they were unsafe and prone to fraud.[9]

Dominion claims they have customers in 28 states using their voting machines. The states that generated the most post-election controversy, however, were Arizona, Georgia, Michigan, Nevada, Pennsylvania, and Wisconsin.[10]

In the weeks following the election, Rudy Giuliani and President Trump's legal team built a case to prove election fraud based on the following serious allegations:[11]

8.   Kyle Olson, Joe Biden touts 'most extensive & inclusive voter fraud organization in history of American politics'
9.   https://www.breitbart.com/2020-election/2020/11/13/top-demo-crats-raised-concerns-about-dominion-voting-technology-in-2019/
10.   https://www.dominionvoting.com/setting-the-record-straight/
11.   https://www.breitbart.com/2020-election/2020/11/19/9-key-points-from-trump-campaign-press-conference-on-challenges-to-election-results/

1. Observers were prevented from watching mail-in ballots being opened.

2. There was unequal application of the law in Democratic counties.

3. Voters arrived at the polls to discover other people had voted for them.

4. Election officials were told not to look for defects in ballots and to backdate ballots.

5. Ballots casting votes for Joe Biden and no other candidates were run several times through machines.

6. Absentee ballots were accepted in Wisconsin without being applied for first.

7. There were "overvotes," with some precincts recording more voters than residents, among other problems.

8. Voting machines and software are owned by companies with ties to the Venezuelan regime and to left-wing donor George Soros.

9. The Constitution provides a process for electing a President if the vote is corrupted.

In conclusion, let's take a look at one of the 6 controversial states: Pennsylvania. According to Pennsylvania's election returns website, President Trump won nearly two thirds of all votes cast in the state on Election Day. Trump received 2.7 million votes—nearly doubling Biden's 1.4 million votes!

Then all hell broke loose. Pennsylvania began counting mail-in ballots. Nobody knew how many votes were still out there by the end of election night, but they just kept counting and counting ... for three more days!

Today the state is reporting more than 2.5 million mail-in ballots—a number never seen before in Pennsylvania. The President's 675,000 vote lead was eroded and eventually the state ceded the election to Biden.

Did Biden really win 2 million of the 2.5 million mail-in ballots? It does seem doubtful. Can you explain why Republicans were not allowed to observe the counting of these votes? Democrat leaders went against the Pennsylvania Constitution and committed several injustices like this against the people of Pennsylvania, and ultimately the American people!

The same story has played out again and again in other Democrat controlled cities and states as well.[12]

---

12.   https://www.thegatewaypundit.com/2020/11/shocking-exclusive-caught-pennsylvania-results-show-statistically-impossible-pattern-behind-bidens-steal-caught/

CHAPTER 1

JANUARY 2021:
AMERICA GETS THE SHAFT

Prior to Joe Biden assuming office on January 20th, the US retail gas price was $2.34 per gallon. Nearly one year later, at the time of the writing of this book, the price of gas is $3.39 per gallon![13] In January of 2021, the inflation rate was 1.4. Annual inflation rate in the US accelerated to a whopping 6.8% in November of 2021, the highest since June of 1982.[14]

These harsh economic realities are a direct result of decisions made by the Biden-Harris Regime, and they are directly opposed to the successful "America First" policies of President #45, Donald J. Trump.

Now, let's take a look at key dates during Biden's first month in office.

JANUARY 6 — CAPITOL PUNISHMENT

The "Save America" rally led by President Trump was held in the National Mall just south of the White House. The vast majority of those in attendance maintained a peaceful presence. As speeches were given by President Trump, Rudy Giuliani, Donald Trump, Jr., Eric Trump, Mo Brooks (R-AL), Rep. Madison Cawthorn (R-NC), and other key Republican

---

13.   https://ycharts.com/indicators/us_gas_price
14.   https://tradingeconomics.com/united-states/inflation-cpi

leaders, the crowds cheered and waved their American flags proudly.

Afterwards, there was a crowd ambling toward the capitol building from the National Mall about 0.3 miles away. Federal officials estimate that about ten thousand protestors from different walks of life entered the Capitol grounds, and more than 800 entered the building.[15]

What started out as a patriotic rally ended in tragedy. Ashli Babbit, a 35-year-old Airforce veteran was shot and killed by a Capitol Police officer. Several protestors and 138 police officers were injured, of whom 15 were hospitalized, some with severe injuries. The Left's retelling of the events surrounding this day has been recorded in history as a right-wing riot, an insurrection instigated by Donald Trump himself.

But who was really behind the violence and destruction on January 6th?

We now have evidence that any violence from the gathering was actually instigated by left wing plants seeking to discredit Trump and the patriots who gathered to protest their concerns over potential election fraud.

The FBI arrested BLM member John Sullivan as one of the leaders of violence committed inside the Capitol that

15.   https://www.washingtonpost.com/politics/2021/02/25/joe-biden-live-updates/#link-SASQGWOOPVHTJBSYQPIR2K-SASQ

day. Sullivan is a twenty-seven-year-old resident of Utah. Based on publicly available information and information provided by Sullivan in an interview on January 7, 2021, described further below, Sullivan is the leader of an organization called Insurgence USA through which he organizes protests.

The federal government obtained a YouTube video of Sullivan, in which, while attending a protest in Washington, D.C., he can be seen telling a crowd over a microphone,

> "We about to burn this sh** down... We got to rip Trump out of office... F--king pull him out of that sh** ... we ain't waiting until the next election ... we about to go get that mother****er." Sullivan then can be seen leading the crowd in a chant of, "It's time for a revolution."[16]

Rep. Mo Brooks, one of the speakers at the "Save America" rally, received left-wing death threats. As a previous victim of left-wing violence, he wore a bulletproof vest on Jan 6 because of BLM and Antifa threats, not conservatives, and spoke out when this was misconstrued:

> "On January 6, at the Ellipse rally, which is one-and-a-half miles from the United States Capitol, I wore an armored vest, a bulletproof vest — although technically, they're not really bulletproof, but they help — and I wore it because the socialist left-wing

16.   https://michaelsavage.com/blm-thug-arrested-for-lead-ing-capital-violence/

radicals in society have uttered any number of
threats of violence — to include death — against
members of the United States Congress, including
myself."[17]

There's no question that Big Tech –– controlled by Leftists
–– aided and abetted the events of January 6th. Social media
algorithms determine what shows up in our news feeds.
They control the reach of any particular post on a given
platform. When questioned by a CNN anchor, the Facebook
VP for Global Affairs and Communications could not rule
out that Facebook may have amplified the tragic events of
Jan 6th. [18]

Since the events of January 6, 727 people have been arrested
and charged with crimes. 151 have entered "guilty" pleas
thus far[19] and nearly 40 are behind bars.[20]

There is evidence, however, that January 6 protesters are
being used as an example. Republican lawmakers received
reports of protestors being mistreated in jail and are being
denied access to investigate.

17.   https://www.breitbart.com/radio/2021/10/29/mo-brooks-wore-bulletproof-vest-january-6-threats-blm-antifa/
18.   https://www.breitbart.com/clips/2021/10/10/facebooks-clegg-on-amplifying-january-6-cant-say-yes-or-no/
19.   https://www.insider.com/all-the-us-capitol-pro-trump-riot-arrests-charges-names-2021-1
20.   https://www.wusa9.com/article/news/verify/capitol-riot-are-hundreds-of-defendants-still-in-jail/65-dffb1d7e-089a-4406-ae4e-c54748e11953

The question remains: Are there January 6 protesters being kept as political prisoners without due process?

> "We still need to know: do we have political prisoners here in America, or not? And we can't get an answer," said Rep. Louie Gohmert (R-TX). "People, whether they've done right or wrong, they deserve to be treated properly." [21]

One Congressional Candidate claims Jan. 6 protestors are actively being denied due process. He warns that regardless of whether one agrees with the protestors, the alleged due process violations impact all Americans. During the Justice for January 6 rally in D.C., Retired Green Beret and Gold Star husband and congressional candidate Joe Kent said,

> "We believe in this country, we believe in this flag. We believe in everything that it stands for, and when there is an injustice done to our fellow citizens and their constitutional rights are taken, if we do not speak out against that, we are guilty of standing by and watching those rights erode. Make no mistake what governments overseas they will do over here, and they have already started...It's banana republic stuff when political prisoners are arrested and denied due process." [22]

---

21.   https://www.breitbart.com/politics/2021/07/28/gop-law-makers-demand-answers-january-6-protesters-political-prisoners-america/

22.   https://www.breitbart.com/politics/2021/09/19/slippery-slope-joe-kent-decries-erosion-january-6-protesters-right-due-process/

It is traditional for the outgoing President to attend the swearing-in of the incoming President.

However, President Trump became the fourth President in U.S. history to skip the inauguration, leaving for Mar-a-Lago in Florida instead. Having raised concerns that the election was stolen from him through electoral fraud, it's hard to blame him.

JANUARY 14 – THE SWAMP MONSTER

Biden revealed a $1.9 trillion stimulus bill intended to combat "a crisis of deep human suffering." The stated goals of the stimulus were to help those who have been financially impacted by COVID, and to speed up vaccine production.

The stimulus, signed in March, provided $1400 to every eligible American, extended unemployment benefits, provided housing assistance, and (a lot) more "pork."

In an interview with Fox & Friends, Senator Tom Cotton (R-AR) slammed the bill, saying it is nothing more than "the swamp looking after itself!"

> "One reason I think Joe Biden thinks there's no time to waste is that Democrats can see cases have plummeted since early January," he said. "They can see that we now have three effective vaccines, and vaccination rates are surging. So, I think they're worried they won't have the coronavirus as an excuse to pay off all of their clients and patrons in a $1.9

trillion blowout bill. As you said, less than a dime of every dollar goes to the coronavirus."

"Just take a look at the payoff of some of their constituencies, $350 billion for states that are poorly run and that have long-standing problems but didn't even lose money because of the coronavirus, places like California and New York," Cotton continued. "A hundred and thirty billion dollars for schools but only a nickel of that money — of each dollar of that money is going to be spent this year. Most of it is for future years. Again, paying off teachers' unions."

"And then maybe the worst of all, the worst of all, they're going to give a lot of Americans a $1,400 check," he added. "Federal employees are going to get that same check. They are also going to get $1,400 a week — a week, every single week if their kids aren't in school. So, if you're working in the middle of the country, hard to make a living, you get one $1,400 payment once. If you're a federal bureaucrat in Washington, where your schools are still closed, you get it every single week. Talk about the swamp looking after itself." [23]

JANUARY 19 – COMMANDER IN THIEF?

Data from a German server indicates the results of the Election as 410-128 for Trump and seem to verify that the election was rigged.

---

23.   https://www.breitbart.com/clips/2021/03/01/sen-cotton-pelosis-1-9-trillion-stimulus-bill-swamp-looking-after-itself/

@TeamSidney posted on Parler,

> "This is the actual results of the election. People in Germany saw this before Dominion servers were seized. This will probably get removed so share as much as possible. The fraud is massive. Shame on these people."[24]

JANUARY 20 – THIRD TIME IS THE CHARM

After three attempts to win the Presidency, Joe Biden was finally successfully installed as the 46th President of these great United States. From his first day in office, it is clear that Biden targeted President Trump's legacy with every action.

His inaugural address promised to 'unite' Americans. He said "Today, on this January day, my whole soul is in this: bringing America together, uniting our people, uniting our nation—and I ask every American to join me in this cause."[25]

While I agree with his goal, nothing has been further from the truth. Biden, like most Democrats, has continued to use identity politics and excessive government overreach to pit Americans against each other for political gain.

---

24. https://newswithviews.com/sydney-powell-has-found-the-actual-results-of-the-Presidential-election/
25. https://en.wikisource.org/wiki/Joe_Biden%27s_Inaugural_Address

(After record-high gas prices and inflation through the roof, Biden ended his first year with 43% approval ratings and chants of "Let's Go, Brandon," so maybe he succeeded in uniting us after all! [26])

Biden doesn't have unilateral control over everything in our nation, but where he does, he lost no time in forcing Americans to wear masks 24-7. His first executive order, 13991, implemented a federal mask mandate, requiring compliance with CDC guidelines in federal buildings and on federal property. Big government thrives on control and limiting individual liberty. [27]

On his first day in office, Biden signed an executive order for the U.S. to rejoin the Paris Agreement, an international agreement claiming to fight climate change, but actually puts America at a serious disadvantage in the global economy.

President Trump originally withdrew the U.S. from the Paris Agreement because it was costly and ineffective, a waste of taxpayer money, and it was bad for our energy competitiveness.[28]

26.   https://news.gallup.com/poll/358343/joe-biden-job-approval-rating-steady-december.aspx
27.   https://www.ctvnews.ca/health/coronavirus/biden-s-first-executive-order-will-require-masks-on-federal-property-1.5274570
28.   https://www.heritage.org/environment/commentary/4-reasons-trump-was-right-pull-out-the-paris-agreement

Biden also revoked a vital permit for the Keystone XL oil pipeline project and issued a moratorium for oil and gas leasing activities in the Arctic National Wildlife Refuge.[29]

Mike Sommers, President and CEO of trade group American Petroleum Institute, said Biden's executive order "is a slap in the face to the thousands of union workers who are already a part of this safe and sustainable project....This misguided move will hamper America's economic recovery, undermine North American energy security, and strain relations with one of America's greatest allies."

Even the Wall Street Journal editorial board concluded it was destructive to the U.S. economy and probably illegal.[30]

Continuing to undermine President Trump's accomplishments, Biden halted construction of the southern border wall with an executive order removing funding. As the grandson of Italian immigrants, I have gone on record that I am pro-immigration. I believe that there should be a faster way for those would make great citizens to become Americans.

However, the Biden-Harris Regime has allowed 200,000+ unvetted and illegal immigrants to cross our borders every month since he took office. This means human and drug

29.   https://financialpost.com/pmn/business-pmn/biden-set-to-rejoin-paris-climate-accord-impose-curbs-on-u-s-oil-industry-5
30.   https://www.breitbart.com/2020-election/2021/01/21/american-workers-business-leaders-on-biden-axing-keystone-pipeline-slap-in-face-to-union-members/

traffickers, terrorists, and other criminals are not being stopped.

You'd think there would at least be some form of forced quarantine, testing, or requirement for vaccination for those crossing our borders illegally — but no, this government has mandated such for legal citizens, not those who come from other countries without proper vetting or legal processing.[31]

Biden also reversed a travel ban that targeted countries with a history of Islamic extremism.[32] The Left purports to be inclusive and accepting by allowing the enemies of America across our borders but is already taking measures to limit the civil liberties of unvaccinated Americans.

Consistent with his order to stop building the border wall, Biden issued a moratorium on the deportation of illegal immigrants. Thankfully, a Federal judge granted Texas a restraining order preventing enforcement because Biden failed "to provide any concrete, reasonable justification for a 100-day pause on deportations."[33]

Thank God for Texas!

---

31.   https://www.valleycentral.com/news/local-news/migrants-that-test-positive-for-covid-19-are-not-being-forced-to-quarantine/
32.   https://www.cnn.com/2021/01/20/politics/executive-actions-biden/index.html
33.   https://apnews.com/article/joe-biden-immigration-texas-barack-obama-51688033e490d50867e52ef9c8ec574f

Additionally, and perhaps the most egregious activity of Inauguration Day 2021, was the complete vanishing act that occurred on the White House website within minutes of the conclusion of the official activities.

President Trump had commissioned an advisory committee of learned historians, scholars, commentators, and analysts to produce an historic response to the claims of the 1619 project, in order to restore understanding of the greatness of the founding of America.

Known as the 1776 Commission, they produced a beautiful full-color report with their findings, and this report was provided on the White House website, ahead of a planned investigation into schools using the 1619 project. [34]

Within moments of the inauguration, the report vanished from the White House website, an attempt to erase history from the modern scholar.

One of the many Executive Orders Biden would stroke his signature to that day dissolved the 1776 Commission.[35] It was only through sheer foresight that we were able to obtain a copy of the 1776 Report prior to White House censorship and make it available in print form as both a paperback booklet and a hardback coffee table book.

---

34.   https://www.cnn.com/2020/09/06/politics/trump-education-department-1619-project/index.html
35.   https://www.cnn.com/2021/01/20/politics/biden-rescind-1776-commission-executive-order/index.html

JANUARY 25 – NOT THE SAME MAN

Biden has long been known as a gaffe machine. But his recent behavior has caused many to question his mental status. Former White House stenographer, Mike McCormick, who worked closely with Biden previously says he is not the same man and "Biden has lost 50% of his cognitive abilities"[36]

Biden signed an executive order that overturned President Trump's ban on transgender individuals serving in the U.S. military. [37]

JANUARY 26 – THE BUSY BEAVER

In his first six days in office, Biden signs 28 executive orders, dwarfing his predecessors with top-down legislation devoid of joint party assessment and acceptance.[38]

If Biden is operating with half of his cognitive ability, then who is really behind all of these executive orders? Barrack Hussein Obama? Kamala Harris? George Soros? Or someone even more sinister?

36.   https://warroom.org/2021/01/25/biden-has-lost-50-of-his-cognitive-abilities/

37.   https://www.whitehouse.gov/briefing-room/Presidential-actions/2021/01/25/executive-order-on-enabling-all-qualified-americans-to-serve-their-country-in-uniform/

38.   https://www.dailywire.com/news/biden-signs-a-whopping-28-executive-orders-dwarfing-his-predecessors

CHAPTER 2

FEBRUARY 2021: AMERICA LAST

As we enter Biden's second month in office, several of his actions seem to prove that he favors citizens of other countries more than the US citizens who supposedly elected him in greater number than any President before him!

FEBRUARY 2 – STRANGERS IN THE LAND

Biden boldly rescinds a Trump memo which required illegal aliens to reimburse the government if they received public benefits intended for US citizens and paid for by US tax dollars.[39] With the national debt at nearly $30 trillion, does this make sense?

It would only make sense if you are a globalist with no concern for the country that supposedly elected you. As a compassionate conservative, however, my heart goes out to these immigrants, illegal or not. But that does not mean that US citizens should be taxed to pay for the benefits of the citizens of another country!

Rather, I believe the Church, instituted by Jesus Christ should lead the way in helping the poor, sick, and needy such as these.

---

39.   https://www.cnn.com/interactive/2021/politics/biden-executive-orders/

"When a stranger resides with you in your land, you shall not wrong him. The stranger who resides with you shall be to you as one of your citizens; you shall love him as yourself, for you were strangers in the land of Egypt" (Lev. 19:33-34).

When the government takes this responsibility from the Church, it renders the Church irrelevant and practically impotent in society. The Church should provide aid, not taxpayers.

FEBRUARY 4 – ICE, ICE, BIDEN.

Biden expands the United States Refugee Admissions Program and rescinds Trump-era policies that limited refugee admissions and required additional vetting. He also issues a memo that directs agencies to ensure LGBTQ+ asylum seekers have equal access to protections.[40]

Thankfully, ICE agents resist Biden's lax attitude toward illegal immigration. Instead, they enforce the law and continue deporting people who are in the US illegally.

> "There are people in ICE that agree with Trump's policies," said Tom Homan, an immigration hard-liner who served as Mr. Trump's ICE director. "They want to do the job they took an oath to do."[41]

---

40.   https://www.cnn.com/interactive/2021/politics/biden-executive-orders/
41.   https://www.nytimes.com/2021/02/03/us/politics/biden-trump-immigration.html

Again, this is a huge opportunity for The Church to step in with solutions specific to the issue of illegal immigration. A civil government is simply not qualified, nor can it truly care about the souls it seeks to salve with benefits instead of The Gospel.

FEBRUARY 10 – PLAYING THE RACE CARD

Biden visits Pentagon for the first time as President. In a speech, he promised never to politicize the military. In the same speech, he emphasized the achievements of Black military service members and called for greater representation at all levels.[42]

Despite the fact that our country fought a war that resulted in the complete abolishment of slavery and has since passed hundreds of laws that level the playing field for all, the Left is always looking for racism behind every corner.

I am not denying that racism still exists. Sure. It exists in many segments of society. But as actor Morgan Freeman so eloquently stated on his interview with CNN anchor Don Lemon, "Making it [racism] a bigger issue than it needs to be is the problem here." Think about it... Here are two successful Black men on national television who have both reached the highest levels of society in a nation that is supposedly still racist.

---

42.   https://www.reuters.com/article/us-usa-biden-defense-idUSKBN2AA2X2

The Biden-Harris Administration may have visited the Pentagon to play the race card, but the elephant in the room was the standard round of defense cuts that usually follow a Democrat put in office.

FEBRUARY 16 – SCREW THE KIDS

In Times Square, a billboard sponsored by the Job Creators Network reads, "Hey Joe—We thought you were going to listen to the science, not special interests. OPEN SCHOOLS NOW. Alfredo Ortiz, JCN President and CEO, said in a statement,

> "Joe Biden's own CDC Director said it's safe to reopen schools, even if teachers have not been vaccinated. Yet the White House has distanced itself from those comments and has failed to full-throatedly endorse a return to in-person classroom instruction...It's clear that Biden is siding with special interests and kowtowing to the teacher's unions, rather than the well-being of our country's children. American schools need to reopen now, and Biden should use the bully pulpit to make it happen."

Biden is catering to Teachers' unions who have resisted opening schools and pushed for more funding for further measures of "safety" before reopening schools.[43]

---

43.   https://www.breitbart.com/politics/2021/02/16/job-creators-network-billboard-demands-biden-stop-siding-with-unions-and-push-to-reopen-schools-now/

Even liberal New York Times says Biden's plan for a return to schools is driven by fear, not the science. Children are less likely to contract or spread the virus, while there are real consequences for children being denied in-person learning and being isolated, masked, and devoid of basic human interactions.

Timothy P. Carney writes,

> "Teachers are understandably scared. After all, school kids are not known for avoiding germs and following every rule. But fear is different from science. The science tells us that schools can be opened safely and that kids need in-person school. Mr. Biden said he would let the science speak, and it's time for him to listen."[44]

FEBRUARY 17 – TWO MASKS ARE BETTER THAN ONE

Biden is photographed wearing two masks in the Oval Office to demonstrate his commitment to stopping the spread of COVID. The CDC has said that wearing 2 masks may help to further reduce the spread of the virus via droplets, but also may make it hard to breathe.

Does anyone else think the incessant virtue signaling is spiraling out of control here? How many times have Democrats been caught without masks when they believed they were in a private setting, sans the press? It has

---

44.   https://www.nytimes.com/2021/02/19/opinion/coronavirus-schools-biden.html.

happened more times than we can count and include in this book. Their elitist motto continues... Freedom for me, but not for thee. [45]

FEBRUARY 17 – HYPOCRISY AT THE HIGHEST LEVEL

Biden presented himself as a moderate, unifying figure. However, he barred President Trump from receiving the intelligence briefings given to every other living former President, claiming Trump could not be trusted.[46]

This attitude is consistent with most democrats who preach acceptance toward anyone but conservatives; who approve of violence if comes from the Left; who shut down economies and strip civil liberties over COVID, but still support and defend the killing of innocent unborn children; who tax citizens to support illegal immigrants; who promote any religion except Christianity; who demand free speech for themselves but not for those who disagree.

The list goes on and on and the hypocrisy is nauseating.

FEBRUARY 18 – REPLACING AMERICA'S REPUBLICAN VOTERS WITH NEW DEMOCRAT VOTERS

Congressional Democrats introduce Biden's plan to offer "path to citizenship" for millions of illegal immigrants

45.   https://www.breitbart.com/politics/2021/02/17/joe-biden-now-wearing-double-masks-in-the-oval-office/
46.   https://www.nytimes.com/2021/02/05/us/politics/biden-trump-intelligence-briefings.html

already in the United States. The plan also eliminates restrictions on family-based immigration and expands worker visas.[47]

America is a diverse country built through many decades of hard work by generations of immigrants like my grandparents – and very likely yours. These immigrants came to America to become members of "one nation, under God, indivisible, with liberty and justice for all."

It was their love for American ideals and their pursuit of the American Dream that brought them together to form a society that would become what we today often refer to as a melting pot.

My great-grandfather, Luigi Vallorani, left his home in Italy for America because he believed the streets here in the New World would be paved with gold. After he survived the Italo-Turkish war and left the military, he knew he did not want to scratch a living from the rocky mountain terrain of Marche like the rest of his farming family.

When he arrived in the US, however, he quickly learned the truth about the streets of America. Not only were they not paved with gold, it was the Italians who were doing the paving! Undaunted by challenges and hardships, Luigi worked hard in the steel mills and coal mines of Pennsylva-

47.   https://www.nytimes.com/live/2021/02/18/us/joe-biden-news#congressional-democrats-roll-out-bidens-immigration-plan-offering-an-eight-year-path-to-citizenship

nia and Kentucky, alongside many others from a myriad of countries who had also migrated here to make a better life.

Saving every penny to get him closer to his goals, eventually Luigi opened and operated a restaurant and a grocery store—bringing the riches of his culture to the American economy.

Like most immigrants during this time in America's history, Luigi was processed quickly upon arrival and immediately considered to be an American. He embraced his American citizenship with pride and committed to learn all about his new nation — its history, language, laws, and culture. His goal was to assimilate as quickly as possible.

Although assimilation had its challenges, this was a great time in American history. People put a high priority on being an American rather than just exploiting their ethnicity for personal gain. The American flag was respected, not burned. People stood proudly for the nation anthem, rather than knelt in protest.

While communities were often knit together in segments of Old-World commonality, it was ultimately patriotism and religion that brought ethnic varietals together, as evidenced by the varied mix most of us find when we process a DNA test. Communities banded together to help each other in times of need.

None of my immigrant ancestors would have taken a dollar from the government. It would have been against their principles. Their attitude was a simple, "No thanks. We earn our own, and we take care of our own." We've lost a lot of that sense of self-reliance and replaced self-governance with handouts and bailouts.

Immigration looks much different today as well. Illegal immigrants are breaching our southern border, exploiting the American catch-and-release loophole by claiming asylum, and adding themselves to the millions already living here illegally.

Those who try to enter legally must often wait years and years, spending thousands of dollars and even hours, navigating an unwieldy maze of documentation and red tape. Even then there are no guarantees of citizenship. I have met people from all over the world—not just Latin America but also Ireland, Australia, and Canada—who simply cannot start the new life they dream of having in this country despite the value they could bring all because of long-standing government policy that I believe needs reform. But I also believe reform can only be achieved when security is first established.

Few politicians or political parties have properly articulated a sound plan for immigration that is efficient while also ensuring the safety of the current citizenry. Republicans want immigrants to follow the law, despite the fact that we lack the resources to enforce those laws. Democrats call for open borders, granting amnesty to immigrants who arrive illegally, and subsidizing them with taxpayer dollars. Why?

The answer is simple. Democrats want to replace America's Republican voters with new Democrat voters from third world countries. It all began with Ted Kennedy's Immigration Act of 1965. Ann Coulter exposed their frightening agenda when she said,

> "Most Americans don't realize that, decades ago, the Democrats instituted a long-term plan to gradually turn the United States into a Third World nation. The country would become poorer and less free, but Democrats would have an unbeatable majority!
>
> Under Teddy Kennedy's 1965 immigration act, our immigration policy changed from one that replicated the existing ethnic population to one that strictly favored unskilled immigrants from the Third World. Since 1968, 85 percent of legal immigrants have come from what is euphemistically called "developing countries."[48]

Democrats need voters because true red-blooded right-leaning salt-of-the-earth Americans won't give them enough votes to win. They've been caught casting ballots on behalf of deceased voters, bribing and bussing voters to the polls, voting multiple times, and even manufacturing votes

---

48.   https://www.appeal-democrat.com/ann-coulter-demography-is-destiny-for-democrats/article_cddf3222-33f0-59f6-ad37-156e0fe7762c.html

out of thin air. It stands to argue that Democrats will stop at nothing to win: even if it requires manipulating the system meant to ensure these very things cannot happen.

The hunger for more votes demands that Democrats turn a blind eye to the effects of loose immigration laws: human trafficking, drug trafficking, criminal activity, and even those bent on committing terroristic acts against us.

In 2010 alone, Amnesty International reported that as many as 60% of women and girls are sexually assaulted while attempting to cross our southern border illegally. [49]

Many argue that not all illegal immigrants are criminals, but they ignore a vital point: by entering this country illegally, a crime has already been committed. In 2018, ICE reported out of 158,581 administrative arrests, 66% of the undocumented illegal parties were convicted criminals. Of the 257,085 removed from this country, 57% were convicted criminals.

Further research conducted by the federal government oversight organization, Judicial Watch, indicates that 50% of all crimes were committed near our border with Mexico. The General Accounting Office documents that criminal immigrants have committed 25,604 murders between 2003 and 2009.

---

49.   https://www.amnesty.org/en/latest/news/2010/04/wide-spread-abuse-against-migrants-mexican-e28098human-rights-cri-sise28099/

As of the writing of this book, 200,000 illegal immigrants are entering into our country each month. We understand why they want to live and work in America. After all, we are the greatest nation on earth. In the interest of national security, however, we cannot allow just anyone and everyone to cross our borders unvetted, unchecked, unconcerned.

While there are countless good people attempting to enter our nation in order to better their lives, there are also gangs, criminals, sex-traffickers, and terrorists. Everyone who wants to enter our country must enter legally for the safety of all.

There is also a question of fairness to all immigrants—past and present—who worked and waited and put great effort into legally entering our country and seeking citizenship that is destroyed when illegal entry is ignored –– and even rewarded.

The Democratic platform which insists illegal immigrants receive amnesty and the full benefits of citizenship in the United States without following legal and lawful due process is giving Democrats access to coerce even more votes. It is a blatant attempt to shift the balance of power from the conservative American values that made us great to the quagmires of failed socialist regimes like Venezuela.

Conservatives aren't opposed to immigrants as the liberals would have you believe. This is a straw man argument

created by the left to control the narrative through the
mainstream media. In fact, the vast majority of the legal
immigrants I am acquainted with hold conservative views.
Rather, Conservatives are against *illegal* immigration,
believing that a wall on our southern border is a necessity to
ensure legal entry.

Democrats want you to believe that building a wall is
insane, cruel, and even racist (but of course, they say
everyone and everything is racist). Barack Obama and
Nancy Pelosi supported the wall a mere number of years
before Trump, as did Bill and Hillary Clinton. What
changed? They are against it now because President
Trump—and conservatives—are in support of it.

Jesus says, "When a strong man, fully armed, guards his
own house, his possessions are safe." (Luke 11:21 NIV) Just
ahead of this verse, He states "Any kingdom divided against
itself will be ruined, and a house divided against itself will
fall." (Luke 11:17 NIV). While Jesus is referring specifically
to spiritual matters in these passages, the principle can be
applied to all areas of our society.

If we are going to move America past these divisive issues,
we must have a new immigration policy that is humanitarian and Biblical. The new policy must respect and
secure our borders and the rule of law, while giving skilled
and motivated people in other nations the opportunity
to become citizens easily. Citizens who contribute to our

economy and have the opportunity to pursue and achieve the American dream for themselves and their families will boost our economy and our overall well-being.

When President Trump was elected, he knew that America was standing at a critical crossroads. The road offered by the Democrats simply kicks the can down the road to future generations. Ironically, just like the city of Troy opening its gates to the Trojan horse, Democrats will be voted out of office by the children of the very people they allowed into our nation.

The second road is dominated by fear of those who are different and leads to an unbiblical xenophobia.

The third road is mutually beneficial to the current citizens and to those who seek to become legal citizens. It is a return to the "Glory Days" of America being a city on a hill, a beacon of hope to thousands across the globe.

In 2024, we need a new President who will enforce our laws, secure our borders, work with other countries to eliminate illegal immigration, and create a new system which welcomes skilled immigrants and temporary workers to improve our economy.

I implore our leaders and our country's citizens to welcome immigrants into this country, legally and efficiently, with reasonable requirements: understand and agree to uphold the Constitution of the United States, honor its laws, create income through gainful employment or building a business, pay taxes, commit to learning our language, and peacefully and lawfully integrate into our society.

Those who come with a hatred for America or wish to overthrow our government or harm our citizens, however, should be forever barred.

Our country is as strong as it is today because our immigrant ancestors risked everything to come here and were more than willing to work hard to make their dreams come true. The American Dream is still alive and well. I believe this is what makes—and will keep—America great.

Of course, America is a work in progress. She has learned from earlier mistakes such as slavery and the mistreatment of Native Americans, and we are still self-correcting. Ultimately it has been our belief in God and our God-given rights that has and will continue to guide us into becoming a better nation through the times.

FEBRUARY 19 – AN END TO "AMERICA-FIRST" DIPLOMACY

In an address at the Munich Security Conference, Biden declared an end to "America-First" diplomacy. If the President of the United States is not supposed to champion the interests of Americans, one wonders who might.

He waxed eloquent about the NATO alliance and vowed to honor America's "obligations." Biden declared, "America is back, the trans-Atlantic alliance is back...we are not looking backward."

For the next fifteen minutes, Biden promoted the power of global alliances. This was a direct attack on President Trump but missed the point of President Trump's presidency entirely. President Trump never said, "America Alone." Rather, he said "America First." There's a big difference. But Democrats are too deaf from their own echo chamber to hear or understand this. [50]

FEBRUARY 25 – BETRAYING THE AMERICAN WORKFORCE

Amid an economy still suffering from COVID restrictions, Biden reversed President Trump's pause on new green cards that protected American jobs in the throes of economic strain.

When in office, President Trump stated, "By pausing immigration, we will help put unemployed Americans first in line for jobs as America reopens. So important... It would be wrong and unjust for Americans laid off by the virus to be replaced with new immigrant labor flown in from abroad. We must first take care of the American worker."

One month after Biden took office, he responded with, "To the contrary... it harms the United States, including by preventing certain family members of United States citizens

---

50.   https://www.nytimes.com/2021/02/19/world/
biden-speech-munich-security-conference.html

and lawful permanent residents from joining their families here. It also harms industries in the United States that utilize talent from around the world."

We know what is really going on here folks. President Trump was putting the American workforce ahead of illegal immigrants. The Right considers this commons sense. The Left considers this racist and xenophobic.

I know it's not politically correct to call them illegal immigrants or illegal aliens, but if they crossed our border illegally, they are here illegally. This does not mean that we don't have a heart. Through the Church, Americans should love and care for them. The State, however, must uphold our laws. Without borders, we cease to be a nation.

The bottom line is that Democrats, led by Joe Biden, are committed to building their voter base by facilitating illegal immigration. Rather than force mass deportations, which is practical at this point, Biden is pushing his plan for an 8-year path to citizenship for the more than 11 million immigrants living illegally in our nation. That's up to 11 million more votes for the Democrats. [51]

51.   https://www.nytimes.com/2021/02/24/us/politics/biden-immigration-trump.html

CHAPTER 3

MARCH 2021: THE GAFFE FACTORY

MARCH 3 – STATES' RIGHTS

One of the strengths of America's Federal system is the rights of states to make important decisions on behalf of their residents that might differ from those of other states. This prevents states like New York and California making rules that could harm smaller states with different values.

Ignoring this fundamental understanding of American government, Biden criticized the governors of Mississippi and Texas for lifting statewide mask mandates, calling it "Neanderthal thinking."

Mississippi's Governor Tate Reeves responded to Mr. Biden's "Neanderthal" comment on Twitter,

> "Mississippians don't need handlers. As numbers drop, they can assess their choices and listen to experts. I guess I just think we should trust Americans, not insult them."[52]

MARCH 3 – GAFFE PREVENTION TACTICS

The video feed for a White House virtual event cuts abruptly after Biden offers to take questions from reporters,

---

52.   https://twitter.com/tatereeves/status/1367204994458521616?s=20

in a possible attempt to keep Biden from committing even more gaffes. [53]

It is important to note that 42 days into his first term, Biden is yet to hold a solo press conference. CNN's Jake Tapper Tweeted that Biden's "15 most recent predecessors all held a formal solo press conference within 33 days of taking office." His handlers are terrified of letting him off the leash. [54]

MARCH 4 – LET ME IN, LET ME IN!

A large number of migrants arrive at the US/Mexico border wearing matching Biden T-shirts which say, "Please let us in!"

> "The President is working to process as many as 25,000 asylum seekers who were forced to wait in Mexico under the Trump Administration's 'Remain-in-Mexico' policy under the Migrant Protection Protocol (MPP) program," Fox News reported.[55]

The shirts were provided by Casa de Luz, a Tijuana organization that "provides assistance to people who have migrated."[56]

53.   https://www.breitbart.com/politics/2021/03/03/wh-cuts-feed-joe-biden-asks-questions/
54.   https://twitter.com/jaketapper/status/1367124836674396165?s=20
55.   https://www.dailywire.com/news/large-number-of-migrants-arrive-at-u-s-mexico-border-wearing-biden-t-shirts-please-let-us-in
56.   https://www.snopes.com/fact-check/immigrants-biden-shirts-let-us-in/

The US has historically been generous with allowing legal immigration, but Biden's policies continue to encourage illegal immigration that is harmful to the US and its citizens, and especially our legal immigrants.

MARCH 5 – A KEPT PRESIDENT?

With his mental health continuing to decline, will Biden eventually be hidden from the public eye? News agencies remark that Biden is the first President in 40 years to not have a formal question and answer session with the media by this point in his presidency. Euphemistically termed "extreme message discipline, "it is more likely a strategy to manage Biden's gaffes.[57]

MARCH 7 – BIDEN'S SCHEME TO GET MORE DEMOCRAT VOTERS

Biden signs an executive order directing agencies to "promote and expand access to voter registration and participation." While this sounds like a noble initiative on the surface, and may be on some levels, one cannot help but see this as yet another Democrat scheme to scrap together more votes for their party. [58]

---

57.   https://apnews.com/article/joe-biden-coronavirus-pandemic-34ffb670bddcdeb7f1224b86fe5d37ec
58.   https://www.cnn.com/interactive/2021/politics/biden-executive-orders/ https://www.nytimes.com/2021/03/07/us/politics/biden-executive-order-voting.html

MARCH 8 — DISCRIMINATING AGAINST WOMEN / GIRLS

Biden signs an executive order that ""all students should be guaranteed an educational environment free from discrimination on the basis of sex, including discrimination in the form of sexual harassment, which encompasses sexual violence, and including discrimination on the basis of sexual orientation or gender identity."

Note that one consequence of these sorts of "gender-affirming" policies in schools is the erasure of girls' sports, as boys who identify as girls claim girls' titles, championships, scholarships, and opportunities. [59]

MARCH 11 – BIDEN CREATES A BIZARRE ARMY TO ADMINISTER COVID-19 VACCINES

Biden "dramatically expanded" ways for people to get the COVID vaccine and the people who could administer the vaccines. 950 community health centers, 20,000 pharmacies, and federally run vaccination sites were among the places offering vaccination. They could be administered by dentists, medical students, midwives, optometrists, and even veterinarians! [60]

What's really shocking is that The Department of Health and Human Services is creating a website for people

59.   https://www.cnn.com/interactive/2021/politics/biden-executive-orders/
60.   https://www.avma.org/javma-news/2021-04-15/veterinarians-help-covid-19-vaccine-delivery

interested in volunteering to administer vaccines! The website will help determine if these volunteers are eligible to do so. [61] Nothing could possibly go wrong here....

This book is not meant to be a treatise on COVID-19, its prevention, or treatment. We know it is a real virus. I have had it myself and I have had two family members and some friends pass away from this wicked virus. I am also not going to deal with the efficacy of the vaccine. I have family and friends who have received all boosters, and family and friends who have not. There are plenty of other more qualified people who can address those debates.

One thing is for sure. I absolutely do not agree with forcing a medical procedure on anyone or any form of coercion by threatening to terminate their employment or limit their civil liberties based on their decision either way.

My biggest concern is that the US and ultimately the world is creating two classes of people: those who have been vaccinated and those who have not.

If this dangerous trend continues, the latter will have limited freedom and be treated like outcasts. How is this any different than past (failed) experiments into class-based society?

---

61.   https://www.nytimes.com/2021/03/11/us/biden-expands-vaccine-sites.html

MARCH 18 — WHO'S REALLY THE PRESIDENT?

Biden calls Kamala Harris "President Harris" and does not correct himself. During a speech celebrating the US nearing administration of 100 million COVID-19 vaccine doses, Biden called his Vice President, Kamala Harris, "President Harris." And he kept on talking.

> "Now when President Harris and I took a virtual tour of a vaccination center in Arizona not long ago, one of the nurses on that, on that tour injecting people, giving vaccinations, said that each shot was like administering a dose of hope." [62]

This was neither the first nor the last time Biden has given Harris an oral promotion.

MARCH 19 — A FRAIL PRESIDENT

Biden falls while boarding Air Force One, fueling speculation about his seeming frailty. He stumbled on the steps twice before falling to his left knee. He then pulled himself up and boarded the aircraft, which departed for Atlanta, Georgia. From one witness's camera angle, he fell low enough to disappear on the tarmac stairs. [63]

Even though I do not agree with Biden's politics, I would not wish something like this to happen to anyone in leadership.

62.   https://nypost.com/2021/03/18/biden-calls-kamala-President-harris-during-speech/
63.   https://www.breitbart.com/politics/2021/03/19/watch-joe-

Not only is it embarrassing, but it's also dangerous for a man Biden's age to fall.

The real question here is whether this man is fit for office. I personally do not believe he is physically or mentally equipped to fulfill his duties as our Commander-in-Chief.

MARCH 21 – CATCH AND RELEASE

Biden begins a "catch and release" policy for migrant families without notifying immigration courts or issuing a Notice to Appear. One Customs and Border Protection official warned, "We are creating another entirely different class of aliens we will have to deal with years from now. We will never find most of the aliens once they are released."

While this plan is likely the result of capacity issues at Border Patrol stations, the CBP official concluded "We may be reducing the time it takes to release a family unit but if we encourage more to come once they find out it is quicker here, we'll be in the same boat again."[64]

MARCH 22 – DEPLORABLE CONDITIONS WORSEN

Biden presents himself as a champion for migrants unlike his predecessor President Trump. However, a series of leaked photos shows deplorable conditions of children

---

biden-falls-on-steps-while-boarding-air-force-one/
64.   https://www.breitbart.com/border/2021/03/21/exclusive-biden-begins-immediate-catch-and-release-of-migrant-families-without-court-dates/

being held in South Texas. The Administration will not allow the press or Members of Congress to photograph this harsh reality.

Rather than enforcing the border, lax Leftist policies have made the crisis even worse by giving migrants a false hope. Now they are piling up at the border and our government is not equipped to handle them. [65]

God is the one who establishes nations and rulers. St. Paul the Apostle writes,

> "The God who made the world and everything in it is the Lord of heaven and earth and does not live in temples built by human hands. And he is not served by human hands, as if he needed anything. Rather, he himself gives everyone life and breath and everything else. From one man he made all the nations, that they should inhabit the whole earth; and he marked out their appointed times in history and the boundaries of their lands. God did this so that they would seek him and perhaps reach out for him and find him, though he is not far from any one of us."[66]

As I have mentioned earlier in this book, this border crisis is a real opportunity for the Church to extend the hand of Christ to our fellow man. While it is not the Church's job to secure the border, it *is* our job to care for the poor.

65.   https://www.breitbart.com/border/2021/03/22/leaked-photos-reveal-bidens-detention-cells-for-migrant-children-on-border/
66.   https://www.biblegateway.com/passage/?-

King Solomon wrote, "Whoever is kind to the poor lends to the Lord, and he will reward them for what they have done." (Proverbs 19:17 – NIV)

MARCH 25 – BIDEN COMES OUT FROM HIDING

Waiting longer than any of his predecessors, Biden finally holds his first press conference as President and is "obviously in a state of radical decline." According to Ben Shapiro, his rambling speaking style, sometimes wandering off in the middle of sentences, indicate advanced mental decline. [67]

As evidence of this decline, there were at least four very awkward moments during his first press conference.

First, he said "Oh God, I miss Donald Trump." Yes, so does America.

At another time, he completely lost his train of thought. Meandering he rambled, "So the best way to get something done...if you hold near and dear to you that you, uh, um, like to be able to— anyway— we're going to get a lot done."

Third, while criticizing election integrity bills being considered in states like Georgia and Michigan he proclaimed, "It's sick—This makes Jim Crow look like

search=acts+17%3A24-27&version=NIV

67.   https://www.dailywire.com/podcasts/the-ben-shapiro-show/ep-1223-biden-s-addled-radical-lying-press-conference-2-part-1

Jim Eagle." Nobody knows who Jim Eagle is, but how is ensuring ballots are cast by legal voters "racist?"

Finally, a reporter asked him to commit to letting the press into border facilities crammed with illegal immigrants. He refused, except to make this contradictory statement, "I will commit to transparency as soon as I'm in a position to implement what we're doing right now." "How soon will that be," the reporter asked. "I don't know, to be clear," Biden responded. [68] Clear as mud, Joe.

Biden accused Republicans of restricting voting access, calling it "sick" and "un-American." The measures that Republicans support include mandatory in-person voting and ID laws, which ensure election integrity. We all know why Democrats fight against election integrity. It will make it harder for them to cheat and steal!

You're the one who is being "un-American," Mr. President.[69]

MARCH 29 – MASK UP, AMERICA!

Biden pushes mask mandates in the face of rising cases throughout the US. The CDC warned of "impending doom" from a potential fourth surge of COVID. [70]

68.   https://www.breitbart.com/politics/2021/03/25/joe-bidens-5-most-awkward-moments-during-press-conference-oh-god-i-miss-donald-trump/
69.   https://www.nytimes.com/2021/03/25/us/voting-rights-biden.html https://www.pewresearch.org/politics/2021/04/22/republicans-and-democrats-move-further-apart-in-views-of-voting-access/
70.   https://www.nytimes.com/2021/03/29/us/politics/biden-vi-

Once again, as Christians, it is our responsibility to love our neighbor as we love ourselves. It is not the President's job to close private businesses or take individual liberty away from American citizens.

Preventative measures such as social distancing, wearing masks, vaccines, etc. are all decisions that individuals must make for themselves, their families, churches, and their communities.

MARCH 30 – ONE HUMAN RACE

Biden keeps campaign promise to appoint people from diverse backgrounds to "redefine what it means to be qualified for the federal bench." Biden appointed three African-American women, one Asian-American, the first Muslim federal district judge, and the first woman of color to serve as a federal judge in Maryland. [71]

It's rather ironic that when President George W. Bush nominated a Black woman to the U.S. Court of Appeals for the District of Columbia Circuit in 2003, then Senator Biden vowed to filibuster and kill her nomination.

A working single mother, Janice Rogers Brown was highly qualified and on the short list to become an associate justice of the U.S. Supreme Court. Biden threatened to filibuster a Black woman again. "I can assure you that would be a very,

rus-vaccine.html

71.   https://www.nytimes.com/2021/03/30/us/politics/biden-judg-es.html

very, very difficult fight and she probably would be filibustered," Biden said. Today, Biden calls filibustering a "relic of the Jim Crow era." [72]

Regardless of Biden's hypocrisy, I assume these candidates will make the best judges, and I certainly applaud diversity. However, one of the ways we can begin to overcome any residual racism in this country is to stop categorizing people into races in the first place!

The Left is far too adept at using identity politics to further divide and conquer Americans. We are ready to replace race-based political identities in favor of "one nation (one race) under God."

From a traditional Christian perspective, there are really no separate races because God made all humans from one couple, Adam and Eve. That means we are all related!

Dr. Georgia Purdom, a PhD in molecular genetics from The Ohio State University, writes,

> "The Bible gives us the answers. Although Adam and Eve are often shown to be fair-skinned and blond, this was unlikely. To derive all the different skin shades from one couple, Adam and Eve likely were middle-brown in color. If Adam and Eve had a mixture of "light color" genes and "dark color" genes, then their descendants could have a wide

72.   https://www.aei.org/op-eds/remembering-the-Black-woman-biden-blocked-from-the-supreme-court/

range of skin color from very light to very dark, with most people somewhere between (as seen in the world today). Adam and Eve likely possessed genetic variation for eye shape and other distinguishing characteristics as well.

As people migrated from Babel, different groups became isolated from others and likely married only within their language group. Each group carried a set of physical characteristics as determined by their genes. As they intermarried, certain characteristics would begin to dominate due to the group's small pool of genes. Over time, different people groups displayed distinct physical characteristics. For example, Asians typically have almond-shaped eyes, dark hair, and middle-brown skin, whereas Europeans have round eyes and fair-colored hair and skin.

The term race is often used to classify people based almost solely on physical characteristics. According to evolutionary ideas, these so-called races descended from different ancestors separated by location and time. However, based on biblical history, the term race must be incorrect. We are all one race ("one blood" in Acts 17:26), the human race, descended from two ancestors, Adam and Eve."[73]

In a truly free society, people should be given positions of leadership based on their qualifications and experience rather than on racial, ethnic, or religious classifications.

---

73.   https://answersingenesis.org/racism/one-race/

If the best person for the job is a female African American, then she should be appointed to the position, but not solely because of her gender or race.

One may ask, what do we do about the fact that African Americans have been disadvantaged for centuries? A Christian society, led by the Church, should do whatever is in its power to reverse this social disparity without being racist in the process.

Historically, Christians have opened schools, orphanages, hospitals, etc. to help those in our society who need help. The governments job is to level the playing field. Christian charity and free enterprise will do the rest.

Once again, by correcting our thinking on these issues, we can derive better solutions as a society.

MARCH 31 – INCREASING TAXES

Biden unveils a $2 trillion infrastructure plan. His second legislative initiative, he claims it will be the biggest investment in American jobs since WWII.

- $621 billion for transportation-related infrastructure

- $300 billion for drinking water-related infrastructure, broadband and electric grids

- $300 billion for affordable housing and upgrading schools

- $400 billion would reportedly go toward care for elderly and disabled American

- $580 billion would be used for domestic manufacturing, job training, research and development

He promised that Americans making under $400k per year would not see a tax increase to pay for the plan but proposed an increase in the corporate tax rate —— which will, of course, be passed on to consumers of all economic levels. [74]

74.   https://www.dailywire.com/news/biden-unveils-massive-infra-structure-plan-calls-it-once-in-a-generation-investment

CHAPTER 4

APRIL 2021: A DEMOCRAT, THROUGH AND THROUGH

Biden's actions in April prove he's a Democrat, through and through. From gun control and social justice to liberal talking points and out of control spending, Biden steamrolls over individual liberty and squanders our grandchildrens' future.

APRIL 8 – PENALIZING GUN OWNERS

Biden signed several anti-gun executive orders during a briefing at the White House. He also nominated David Chipman, a gun control lobbyist, to head up the ATF!

Conservatives respond that these actions are unlikely to reduce gun violence and rather they will turn law-abiding gun owners into felons.

Gun homicides are down significantly from the 1990s, even though more and more people own guns. In 2020, 8 million Americans purchased guns for the first time because they care about the safety of their homes and communities. [75]

Why do Democrats pretend to care about gun violence? Simple. Their real agenda is to disarm potential dissenters.

---

75.   https://www.heritage.org/firearms/commentary/heres-why-President-bidens-executive-action-guns-wont-stop-gun-violence

They hate the Second Amendment because it was written to protect us from the kind of power-hungry bureaucrats and politicians they are!

Without the Second Amendment, how will we protect our rights to the First –– and all the rest?

APRIL 9 – TO THE MOON!

Biden proposes a $24.7 billion budget for NASA to fund moon exploration—a $1.5 billion increase over 2021—to fight climate change, and more.

The International Space Station's funding was a separate line item. NASA Acting Administrator Steve Jurczyk stated, "This $24.7 billion funding request demonstrates the Biden Administration's commitment to NASA and its partners who have worked so hard this past year under difficult circumstances and achieved unprecedented success." [76]

I was born four years after the first moon landing and grew up watching Shuttle launches. This era of American prowess in space left an indelible impression on me, and I am all for space exploration. However, I do not believe billions of taxpayer funds should be allocated to "fighting climate change" in space.

---

76.   https://www.space.com/biden-nasa-2022-budget-request

APRIL 14 – AN INEFFECTIVE LEADER REVEALED

Biden announces his plan for American influence to exit Afghanistan by September 11, 2021, on the 20-year anniversary of one of the most tragic events on our nation's soil: the attack of Islamic radicals that resulted in the death of 2,996 in one day.

> "It is time to end America's longest war. It is time for American troops to come home," President Biden said. He claimed that we've spent too much of the taxpayer's money, $1.57 trillion to be exact, which is odd because Democrats could care less about spending our money. Like most Democrat rhetoric, this sounded noble on the surface. But the disaster that eventually ensued by his botched exit left a wake of chaos and destruction. It undermined all the sacrifices made by our men and women over the last twenty years–2,000 of whom gave their lives![77]

APRIL 22 – A CONVENIENT CRISIS

Biden commits to halving US emissions by the end of the decade to fight climate change. Even liberal New York Times admits this ambitious goal "will be extraordinarily difficult to meet, economically and politically."

Experts say that this would require a dramatic overhaul of American society—eliminating coal for producing elec-

---

77.   https://www.cnbc.com/2021/04/14/biden-announces-us-troops-to-leave-afghanistan-by-sept-11.html

tricity and moving from gasoline to electric-powered cars. Russia, China, and India made no commitment to reduce emissions. [78]

When God created humankind, He entrusted them with stewardship of the earth. We are to responsibly cultivate and harvest resources in a sustainable way to advance and grow as a species. This honors our Creator. It's hardwired into our DNA.

As a compassionate conservative, I care deeply about our planet. There are environmental concerns that are well founded and serious. These should not be politicized, pitting right against left. Rather, it should be a moral issue.

Other environmental concerns are without foundation or greatly exaggerated. In these cases, the Left is manufacturing one crisis after another for the sole purpose of scaring the public into turning over more and more of their freedom for security. More government is not the answer. And capitalism without a moral compass can create just as much damage through consumption without concern for future generations.

The Cornwall Declaration on Environmental Stewardship articulates these values the best,

> "Public policies to combat exaggerated risks can dangerously delay or reverse the economic devel-

78.   https://www.nytimes.com/2021/04/22/climate/biden-climate-change.html

opment necessary to improve not only human life but also human stewardship of the environment. The poor, who are most often citizens of developing nations, are often forced to suffer longer in poverty with its attendant high rates of malnutrition, disease, and mortality; as a consequence, they are often the most injured by such misguided, though well-intended, policies. [79]

APRIL 16 – BIDEN AGREES WITH TRUMP

After promising to raise the refugee limit on the campaign trail, Biden instead keeps it at the 15,000-limit instituted by President Trump. The Democrats considered President Trump's limits to be "racist" policy and were in a state of shock over President Biden's decision to maintain President Trump's limits.

Clearly, the crisis of migrant children at the border has the President worried about losing midterm elections. Flights were canceled for over 700 refugees who had already been vetted and issued tickets to travel here.[80]

I certainly believe that America, as a Judeo-Christian nation, should seek to provide sanctuary for those are who are fleeing war, poverty, and natural disasters. Democrats and Republicans cannot agree on a plan that allows

79.   https://cornwallalliance.org/landmark-documents/the-cornwall-declaration-on-environmental-stewardship/
80.   https://www.nytimes.com/2021/04/20/us/politics/biden-refugees.html

immigrants into this country legally and in a way that does not threaten to overwhelm our economy and national security.

Biden announces sanctions on Russia over Solarwind's cyber-attack, which is blamed on Russia's intelligence agency. While Biden does not want to escalate the conflict, Russia called the steps "hostile steps which dangerously raise the temperature of confrontation".[81]

To save face, the Democrats led by Joe Biden are still punishing Russia for what has already been proven to be a hoax of mythical proportions. The alleged Russia collusion theory goes back to the early months of President Trump's first term. Hillary Clinton and her operatives put together a collection of lies and inuendo claiming that Russia interfered in the 2016 election. The media bought it and RussiaGate was born.[82]

The perpetuation of this hoax threatens our international relations with Russia and could have a very dangerous outcome.

APRIL 17 – STANDING UP TO CHINA

Biden receives his first visit from a foreign leader—Japanese Prime Minister Yoshihide Suga. China's activity in the Indo Pacific dominated the agenda of their summit. Biden and

81.   https://www.bbc.com/news/technology-56755484
82.   https://nypost.com/2021/11/04/the-real-collusion-was-the-creation-of-russiagate-out-of-absolutely-nothing/

Suga declared a unified front against Chinese aggression in Hong Kong, Taiwan, and Xinjiang.

The Chinese embassy in DC responded, saying they were "resolutely opposed" to the alliance and that these were China's internal affairs. [83]

APRIL 24 – BIDEN GETS SOMETHING RIGHT

Biden becomes the first President to acknowledge the Turkish killings of Armenians in the 20th century as genocide. "Each year on this day, we remember the lives of all those who died in the Ottoman-era Armenian genocide and recommit ourselves to preventing such an atrocity from ever again occurring," Mr. Biden said in a statement issued on the 106th anniversary of the beginning of a brutal campaign by the former Ottoman Empire that killed 1.5 million people.

"And we remember so that we remain ever vigilant against the corrosive influence of hate in all its forms."[84]

While I applaud President Biden for standing up to Turkey and recognizing this genocide, I also warn him and the Democrat Party that their own policies of forcing medical procedures on American citizens is creating a class of

83.   https://www.cnbc.com/2021/04/17/biden-and-japans-su-ga-project-unity-against-chinas-assertiveness.html
84.   https://www.nytimes.com/2021/04/24/us/politics/arme-nia-genocide-joe-biden.html

"second class" citizens. These are the first steps in a similar and dangerous direction and is anti-American to the core.

APRIL 27 – THE REDISTRIBUTION OF INCOME

Biden increases minimum wage for federal contractors to $15.[85] Much to the dismay of his far-left allies, Bernie Sanders was unsuccessful in his effort to raise the minimum wage to $15 in the private sector earlier this year.[86]

By establishing this raise on the federal level, the Democrats are paving the way for a minimum wage hike across the board.

While I want the quality of life to improve for all Americans, it is dangerous for the government to interfere in the private sector. "The problem with policy makers trying to raise workers' incomes through government mandates is that laws can't create additional income—they can only redistribute it. What relieves one person's struggles increases another's woes—and creates a whole host of unintended consequences," writes Rachel Greszler, Research Fellow in Economics, Budget, and Entitlements at The Heritage Foundation.[87]

85.   https://www.federalregister.gov/documents/2021/04/30/2021-09263/increasing-the-minimum-wage-for-federal-contractors
86.   https://www.breitbart.com/politics/2021/03/05/democrats-rage-as-15-minimum-wage-effort-fails-despicable-unacceptable/
87.   https://www.heritage.org/jobs-and-labor/commentary/15-minimum-wage-worth-the-costs

APRIL 28 – A NEW ERA OR ERROR?

During Biden's first formal address to a joint session of Congress, Biden called for a dramatic increase in the role of the federal government, federal spending, and ultimately a reshaping of American society.

"The rest of the world isn't waiting for us," Mr. Biden said. "I just want to be clear. From my perspective, doing nothing is not an option." This spending has fueled out-of-control inflation throughout his first term.

In the GOP rebuttal, Senator Tim Scott accused Biden of offering empty platitudes and promoting "big government waste." Scott invoked his own experience as a deeply religious Black man who was raised in the south, "Our best future will not come from Washington schemes or socialist dreams; it will come from the American people — Black, Hispanic, white, Asian, Republicans and Democrats," he said. "We are not adversaries. We are all in this together."[88]

---

88. https://www.nytimes.com/live/2021/04/28/us/biden-speech-congress

CHAPTER 5

MAY 2021: THE WORST PRESIDENT SINCE CARTER

MAY 2 – PROMISES BROKEN

After criticism from fellow Democrats over failing to keep his promise to raise the refugee limit, Biden raised it to 62,500. This is far above the 15,000-limit set by President Trump, but not nearly as high as Biden's original promise of 125,000 on the campaign trail.

> "It is important to take this action today to remove any lingering doubt in the minds of refugees around the world who have suffered so much, and who are anxiously waiting for their new lives to begin," said Mr. Biden.

This is in addition to out-of-control illegal entry, all at a time when Americans are struggling economically due to restrictions put in place to combat COVID-19.[89]

MAY 3 – FREE COLLEGE!

Biden makes remarks regarding the American Families Plan, which he originally announced on April 28. The American Families Plan guarantees free universal preschool, subsidized daycare, programs for nutrition, paid

89.   https://www.npr.org/2021/05/03/993216680/biden-raises-refugee-cap-to-62-500-after-earlier-criticism

family leave, and four additional years of public education (college), all without making the deficit worse or raising taxes for non-wealthy people.

Biden promised "Anybody making less than $400,000 a year will not pay a single penny in taxes." Who will cover these expenses, then?

Mr. Biden also claims it will make us more competitive in the race against other nations, "The investment we need to win the competition — the competition with other nations for the future. Because we're in a race. We're in a race." [90]

I find this choice of words to be a strange contradiction, since the Democrats are globalists now. Why are we "racing" to "win" against other nations? If President Trump said this, he would be attacked for being a xenophobe, a nationalist, and all manner of "racism" accusations.

And how can our nation, now nearly $30 trillion in debt already, continue to take on more and more financially? We are creating an unfixable mess for our children and grand-children.

MAY 6 – NO ROOM FOR GOD

Biden releases a statement for the National Day of Prayer –– and completely fails to mention God.

90.   https://www.whitehouse.gov/briefing-room/speeches-re-marks/2021/05/03/remarks-by-President-biden-on-the-american-families-plan/

He did, however, mention racial justice and climate change.[91] Once again, the Democrats are on the wrong side of God and history.

This shouldn't surprise us, however, as Democrats conspicuously removed God from their party platform in 2020. [92] There was "no room in the inn" for our Lord when He was born nearly 2000 years ago either.

Joe Biden supporters love to claim that he is a devout Catholic, but his support of taxpayer-funded abortions as well as establishing laws forcing doctors to perform abortions and transgender surgeries against their will runs in direct opposition of the sacred teachings of the Church.

He did, however, pay rare homage to the First Amendment,

> "The First Amendment to our Constitution protects the rights of free speech and religious liberty, including the right of all Americans to pray. These freedoms have helped us to create and sustain a Nation of remarkable religious vitality and diversity across the generations."

91.   https://www.breitbart.com/faith/2021/05/06/national-day-of-prayer-joe-biden-mentions-racial-justice-climate-change-not-god/
92.   https://www.washingtonpost.com/national/on-faith/democrats-under-fire-for-removing-god-from-party-platform/2012/09/05/61b3459a-f79e-11e1-a93b-7185e3f88849_story.html

MAY 11 — JABBER-IN-CHIEF

Biden holds a bipartisan meeting of State Governors to encourage vaccination.

Present at the virtual meeting, where no reporters were present, were Republican Governors Spencer Cox (Utah), Charlie Baker (Massachusetts), and Mike DeWine (Ohio), as well as Democratic Governors Michelle Lujan Grisham (New Mexico), Janet Mills (Maine) and Tim Walz (Minnesota).

"We have to make it easier and more convenient for all Americans to get vaccinated," Biden said. He encouraged governors to offer incentives to vaccinated citizens.

Ensuring that a large percentage of Americans receive vaccines was seen as the way forward and back to normalcy, before Delta and Omicron variants cropped up that appeared to be more resistant to the vaccine. [93]

MAY 12 — HIGHEST GAS PRICES SINCE OBAMA ADMINISTRATION

Due to Biden's energy policies and exacerbated by a cyber-attack on the Colonial Pipeline, gas prices reached their highest level since Obama's presidency.

---

93.   https://www.pbs.org/newshour/politics/watch-live-biden-meets-with-state-governors-to-discuss-vaccination-programs

The national average is $3.008 compared to $2.99 under Obama in 2014, making it the highest price point in 6.5 years. [94]

More than a thousand gas stations across North Carolina, South Carolina, Tennessee, Georgia, and southern Virginia ran out of gas due to a disruption in the supply chain. The disaster, which comes less than a week after a dismal U.S. jobs report, caused many Americans to compare Joe Biden's presidency to that of former President Jimmy Carter.

How can middle-class America simultaneously struggle to pay for these sky-rocketing prices and a waning job market?

MAY 19 – INSPIRED BY A CHINESE DICTATOR

Biden gives a speech at the Coast Guard commencement ceremony, during which he botches a quote from genocidal Communist Dictator, Mao Zedong.

Before we get to the actual quote, let that sink in: The President of the United States of America is quoting Chairman Mao—a Communist Dictator responsible for an estimated 80 million executions during his brutal totalitarian regime—but c'mon man, he's got some real wisdom!

Specifically, Biden misquoted "Women hold up half the sky" as "women hold up half the world." He uses this quote often, such as when he announced Kamala Harris as his

94.   https://www.dailywire.com/news/national-average-gas-price-surges-to-highest-level-since-obama-era

running mate, and sometimes refers to it as a Chinese proverb. [95]

No, Biden. It's simply a Communist dictator's thought.

As if this were not enough, he also lifted and botched a joke originally told by President Reagan at a similar commencement address to the Coast Guard class of 1988.

President Reagan said: "My Coast Guard aides have been excellent. One of them taught me that that the Coast Guard is that hard nucleus about which the navy forms in time of war." The joke generated a big cheer and lots of laughter.

Here's Biden's botched version: "I can only assume that you'll enjoy educating your family about how the Coast Guard is, quote, the hard nucleus around the Navy forms in times of war."

The class of 2021 did not laugh, which prompted Biden to respond by saying, "You are a really dull class." [96]

Biden has a history of plagiarism, gaffes, and insults, and they continue to worsen as his mental state declines.

95.   https://www.breitbart.com/politics/2021/05/19/joe-biden-botches-quote-from-communist-dictator-mao-zedong-during-coast-guard-commencement-speech/
96.   https://www.dailymail.co.uk/news/article-9598795/Presidents-Coast-Guard-joke-left-dull-class-groaning-cracked-REAGAN-1988.html

MAY 24 – ACTIONS SPEAK LOUDER THAN WORDS

Over 500 former Biden campaign staffers urge Biden to hold Israel responsible for the Israeli-Palestinian crisis. [97]

While the purpose of this book is not to present a treatise on Israel-Palestine relations, a few things need to be addressed.

First, Israel returning to the land of their ancestors after millennia of dispersion and being recognized as a nation in 1948 started the modern conflict with historic Palestine. Does the land belong to Israel or Palestine?

A common Evangelical Christian view is that the Jews returning to the land God gave to Abraham is a fulfillment of Biblical prophecy.

Palestinians believe that because they were in most recent control of the land, that it should stay in their possession.

The Left sides with Palestine and the Right sides with Israel. Strangely enough, the Left wails over the conquerors of old who came here! In an attempt to––at best whitewash and at worst erase–– history, the Left bemoans and berates the arrival of Spanish and English explorers on land the Native Americans called theirs.

---

97.   https://matan-aradneeman.medium.com/dear-President-biden-b19600918a67

During his presidency, Donald Trump recognized Jerusalem as the true capital of Israel, which enraged the Left. Ironically, isn't it the Left that is always pointing a finger at anti-Semitism and racism?

The Left is also pushing for further gun control measures in the United States, which disarms Jewish people and prevents the ability to protect themselves against terrorist attacks and hate crimes against them, something that is 2.2-2.6 times more likely to happen. [98] They've catered to Muslim beliefs and laws in many parts of the country. [99] Some Jewish people believe that there is real evidence of bias towards Muslims in the US. [100]

Whether there is or not is not something we are here to debate, but it does seem odd that in a country that should not respect one religion over another we have such anger from the Left over the Jewish people claiming Israel.

Biden put out an official statement against anti-Semitic remarks, but his actions as well as the actions of the Left are truly anti-Semitic. [101]

---

98. https://www.aei.org/carpe-diem/based-on-2019-fbi-data-jews-were-2-6x-more-likely-than-Blacks-and-2-2x-more-likely-than-muslims-to-be-victims-of-hate-crimes/
99. https://detroit.cbslocal.com/2015/11/04/detroit-enclave-to-have-what-will-be-muslim-majority-council/
100. https://www.nbcnews.com/news/us-news/laura-loomer-banned-uber-lyft-after-anti-muslim-tweetstorm-n816911
101. https://www.whitehouse.gov/briefing-room/statements-re-leases/2021/05/28/statement-by-President-joe-biden-on-the-rise-of-anti-semitic-attacks/

MAY 24 – FOLLOW THE MONEY

Biden and Fauci host a YouTube town hall to encourage young Americans to get vaccinated. "I know folks have a lot of questions about the COVID-19 vaccines, so Dr. Fauci and I hosted a YouTube Town Hall with Manny Mua, Brave Wilderness, and Jackie Aina to answer them. Make sure to tune in for the premiere."[102]

There's a popular catchphrase from the 1976 docudrama film, *All the President's Men*, that says political corruption can be exposed when you, "Follow the Money."

As I wrote earlier in this book, I am not qualified to say whether the various vaccines are efficacious or not. But it raises serious suspicions when you see Big Government in bed with Big Pharma and asking YouTube stars to help them beg people to get vaccinated.

After all, if the vaccine is that amazing, why don't we see people clamoring and fighting each other in a stampede to get their shots?

During the town hall, Biden promised, "Federally, we are not going to have any mandate." [103]

We hoped he would not break *this* promise.

---

102.   https://twitter.com/POTUS/status/1396859490935447552
103.   https://deadline.com/2021/05/joe-biden-anthony-fauci-you-tube-stars-covid-19-1234763010/

MAY 28 – TAX AND SPEND

Biden proposed a $6 trillion budget plan that would cause US debt to rise to a percentage of the economy higher than that during WWII!

His administration defended the plan saying that the nation needs these expenditures for infrastructure, education, the environment, public health, and social safety-net programs to recover from the pandemic.

Of course, he proposes paying for this plan by taxing corporations and wealthy Americans even more. [104] Taxing corporations and the wealthy ultimately hurts the poor and middle class because the government is limiting the ability for the money to be spent in a free market and tries to redistribute it in a way that punishes productivity.

Once President Trump's tax cuts expire in 2025, Biden is likely to break his campaign pledge and increase taxes on those making less than $400,000 per year. Why not? Democrats seem to love nothing more than to increase taxes and limit freedoms.

---

104.   https://www.usatoday.com/story/news/politics/2021/05/28/bidens-budget-proposal-expected-increase-federal-debt/7468014002/

MAY 28 – CREEPY JOE

Biden was criticized for making "creepy" comments sexualizing an underage girl during a speech at a Virginia military base.

Of course, there are entire video montages that show him sniffing, touching, and making uncomfortable remarks to and about girls––and boys–– on a routine basis.

This particular time he said, "I tell you what, look at her, she looks like she's 19 years old, sitting there like a little lady with her legs crossed." Huh? Why are you looking at her legs, Creepy Joe?

In 2019, Biden issued a statement claiming that he has never acted inappropriately. Democrats rush to Biden's defense saying he means to be sweet. Whatever his intentions are, this behavior should have stopped a long time ago.

We all know that President Trump would be slaughtered in the press for anything like this. [105] It's just simply not even remotely appropriate.

105.   https://www.dailymail.co.uk/news/article-9631457/Creepy-Joe-Biden-slammed-remarks-elementary-school-aged-girl.html

CHAPTER 6
JUNE 2021: RUNAWAY INFLATION

JUNE 1 — THE END OF GAS-POWERED VEHICLES

Biden's decision to cancel the Keystone XL pipeline as well as suspend harvesting gas and oil on government land is haunting him and crippling the U.S. economy in early June.

Unlike President Trump, who wanted energy independence for the United States, Biden's disastrous policies have been particularly noticeable as we see runaway inflation and excessively rising prices. Over Memorial Day weekend, gas sold at nearly $6 a gallon in Los Angeles! [106]

To add insult to injury, California Governor Gavin Newsom pledged to ban the sales of gas-powered vehicles by 2035.

Did you catch that? That's right, ban.

When Biden was the Vice President, he set a deadline for the U.S. to eliminate fossil fuels from production by 2035. This is about five years later than liberal extremist Alexandria Ocasio-Cortez proposed in her "Green New Deal." [107]

---

106.   https://www.breitbart.com/politics/2021/06/01/photo-gas-prices-near-6-per-gallon-in-los-angeles-california/
107.   https://www.breitbart.com/politics/2020/09/23/californi-as-gavin-newsom-bans-gas-powered-vehicles-effective-2035/

The takeaway here is not that electric-powered vehicles are a bad idea. Rather, it's that the free market should be the primary force in this transition. Forcing it on the American people will be detrimental to our economy and hit families the hardest.

At a speech in Tulsa, marking the 100th anniversary of the massacre against the Greenwood District in May 1921 that was compared to the treatment of European Jews during WWII,[108] Biden stated, "According to the intelligence community, terrorism from white supremacy is the most lethal threat to the homeland today," Biden said. "Not ISIS. Not Al Qaeda. White supremacists." [109]

Somehow, I find this hard to believe. 1921? A lot has happened in the last 100 years to eradicate racism in America. And frankly, the last "white supremacy" hate crime splashed across the news cycle was invented out of thin air by actor and singer Jussie Smollett. Since then, Jussie has been convicted of felony disorderly conduct for staging a fake hate crime.[110]

By and large, our country has left racism behind except when the Left drums it up to further divide and conquer our nation.

---

108.   https://www.youtube.com/watch?v=WmZZKCU5Jr0

109.   https://www.breitbart.com/politics/2021/06/01/joe-biden-ter-rorism-from-white-supremacy-the-most-lethal-threat-to-the-home-land/

110.   https://www.npr.org/2021/12/09/1062768250/jussie-smol-lett-verdict

JUNE 2 – BIDEN MAKES RACIST COMMENTS

While speaking in Tulsa, OK, on the afore-mentioned race-related issues, Biden uttered yet another racist gaffe, "The data shows young Black entrepreneurs are just as capable of succeeding given the chance as white entrepreneurs are. But they don't have lawyers. They don't have, they don't have accountants, but they have great ideas. Does anyone doubt this whole nation be better off from the investments those people make? And I promise you that's why I set up this National Small Business Administration that's much broader because they're going to get those loans." [111]

Jeffrey A Dove Jr., a Black Army combat veteran and former Republican congressional nominee tweeted, "Why is it that every time he speaks about the Black community, he makes us seem incapable of the simplest tasks? Whether it's getting an ID card, using the internet to make an appointment or now this." [112]

This is another example of Democrats, especially elitist white ones, getting caught making condescending and patronizing remarks about the Black community. After all, they see themselves as the "white savior."

---

111.   https://www.dailywire.com/news/biden-Black-entrepreneurs-just-as-capable-as-whites-but-they-dont-have-lawyers-or-accountants
112.   https://twitter.com/JefferyADoveJr/status/1399855745441665027

Alternatively, Conservatives evaluate a person based on their work ethic and contribution to society, not their skin color.

Many in the Black community have come to recognize this and speak out against racism from the Left. Unfortunately, they are often quickly labeled as "Uncle Toms," and often marginalized. Thankfully this trend is reversing.

JUNE 6 – HISTORICAL AMNESIA

On the 77th anniversary of D-day, Biden posts a video of himself meeting with survivors of the 1921 Tulsa Massacre. Using his Presidential Twitter account, Biden tweeted, "I met with survivors of the Tulsa Massacre this week to help fill the silence. Because in silence, wounds deepen. And, as painful as it is, only in remembrance do wounds heal."

While this is a noble meeting, failing to mention the largest amphibious invasion in history is more than a massive oversight. It is unpatriotic and unbefitting of a U.S. President. It is an insult to those who laid down their lives that day and liberated a continent from Nazi tyranny.

Biden has a history of confusing important U.S. holidays. In May of 2020, he was criticized for confusing D-Day (June 6) with National Pearl Harbor Remembrance Day (December 7).

Vice President Kamala Harris and even Canadian Prime Minister Justin Trudeau also faced criticism for failing to acknowledge D-Day. Again, we shouldn't be surprised. The Left does not care about our history unless they can use it for some political leverage against their adversaries. They seem to be simply unpatriotic and despise the values and principles that made America the greatest nation in the history of the world.

Once again, their true colors are revealed, and they are not red, white, and blue. [113]

JUNE 12 – FREEDOM FOR ME, BUT NOT FOR THEE!

The G7 (Group of Seven) organization of the world's seven largest advanced economies, specifically, Canada, France, Germany, Italy, Japan, the UK, and the United States met once again in 2021.

At the end of the G7 summit, Biden and the other leaders were photographed without face masks or social distancing. Of course, by this point, good science cast doubt on the efficacy of both measures to prevent the spread of COVID-19.

However, given how often Biden and the Left has insisted –– and mandated –– that Americans must do these things, it's very hypocritical.

---

113.   https://www.dailywire.com/news/biden-neglects-to-com-memorate-d-day-tweets-about-tulsa-massacre-instead

Official photographs were taken of the leaders on the world's stage, all at least 6 feet apart. But once they thought the cameras were off, off came the masks, no more elbow bumps, and out went the social distancing. [114]

This is not the first time that mask-pushing, vaccine-happy, lockdown-hungry Democrats have been caught with their masks down. I'm happy for them to express their freedom, but why do they insist that the rest of us real people live any differently?

Easy answer. This is elitism at its finest. It's "good for me but not for thee!" At least Conservatives are usually more (not always) consistent and rarely get caught exhibiting such blatant hypocrisy. I always caution myself and others, however, not to become too judgmental and remain humble because "but for the grace of God go I."

JUNE 14 – GULAGS AND THE SECRET POLICE

During a White House teleconference, a senior official in the Biden Administration announced plans to create a way for Americans to report friends and family members who have become "radicalized" to combat political violence.

Of course, we all know that the real goal here is to silence political opponents and dissidents.

---

114.   https://www.breitbart.com/europe/2021/06/12/no-masks-no-distancing-disgraceful-covid-hypocrisy-of-the-g7-elite/

"This involves creating contexts in which those who are family members or friends, or co-workers know that there are pathways and avenues to raise concerns and seek help for those who they have perceived to be radicalizing and potentially radicalizing towards violence," said a senior Administration official.

The official also announced a partnership with technology companies to surveil the population, "One of the principal tools now at our disposal is our decision to join the Christchurch Call to Action to Eliminate Terrorist and Violent Extremist Content Online. This is an international partnership between governments and technology companies that works to develop new solutions to eliminating terrorist content online while safeguarding the freedom of online expression.

This should cause a number of alarms to sound in the minds of all Americans, liberal or conservative, who value freedom of speech and individual liberty.

Government programs encouraging people to inform on their neighbors and family members conjures up images of Russian Gulags, Stasi reports, and secret police. Wake up, folks! [115]

---

115. https://www.whitehouse.gov/briefing-room/press-briefings/2021/06/15/background-press-call-by-senior-administration-officials-on-the-national-strategy-for-countering-domestic-terrorism/

JUNE 17 - JUNETEENTH

Biden signs legislation to make Juneteenth a Federal holiday. Originating in Galveston, Texas, June 19th has been observed in various parts of the United States since 1865. It celebrates African-American culture and the end of slavery.

However, during Biden's 36 years in the Senate, he did not sponsor or co-sponsor any Juneteenth bills. Funny how it wasn't important until it became politically expedient! [116] In fact, Biden is notorious for being adamantly against Civil Rights![117] He actually drafted the legislative language used to oppose school integration.

In a 1975 Senate hearing, longtime director of the NAACP Legal Defense Fund, civil rights lawyer Jack Greenberg, took freshman Senator Biden to task over his sponsorship of a bill to limit the power of courts to order school desegregation!

This bill, said Greenberg "heaves a brick through the window of school integration," and according to Greenberg, Biden was the hand that threw the brick.[118]

I am not going to delve into the complex issues surrounding the War Between the States in this book. Suffice it to say

116.   https://www.breitbart.com/politics/2020/06/19/joe-biden-did-not-sponsor-co-sponsor-any-juneteenth-bills-in-senate/
117.   https://www.nbcnews.com/news/nbcblk/joe-biden-didn-t-just-compromise-segregationists-he-fought-their-n1021626
118.   https://www.nbcnews.com/news/nbcblk/joe-biden-didn-t-just-compromise-segregationists-he-fought-their-n1021626

that Abraham Lincoln was a Republican and the South was predominantly Democrat at the time. Jim Crow laws were established and enforced by Democrats.

The Democrat party has a history of holding down the Black community while accusing Republicans of racism. Senator Joe Biden had ample opportunity during his 36 years on Capitol Hill to fight against racism; instead he fought to hold onto it.

Now that he's in the White House (and Corn Pop is watching), it's time to do something truly decent for our fellow Americans of African descent! Way to go, Joe!

JUNE 23 – THREATENING GUN OWNERS

You can't make this stuff up! During a press conference, Biden threatens law-abiding gun owners, saying that if they want to take on the government, they will need nuclear weapons and F-15s. Check this out...

> "The Second Amendment, from the day it was passed, limited the type of people who could own a gun and what type of weapon you could own," Biden said. "You couldn't buy a cannon. [Those who] say the blood of the, the blood of patriots, you know, and all this stuff about how we're going to have to move against the government."

> "Well, the tree of liberty is not [watered with] the blood of patriots, what's happened is that there

never been, if you want, if you think you need to
have weapons to take on the government, you need
F-15s and maybe some nuclear weapons," Biden
continued. "The point is that there's always been the
ability to limit, rationally limit, the type of weapon
that can be owned, and who can own it."

These comments were roundly criticized by journal-
ists, political opponents, and those who believe in the
importance of our Second Amendment rights. [119]

I don't recall the Second Amendment putting limits on the
rights of our citizens to keep and bear arms.

JUNE 24 – WHISPERER-IN-CHIEF

The phrase "Creepy Joe" trends after Biden gave bizarre
press conference on infrastructure where he leaned forward
and whispered into the microphone several times.

> When asked about the timeline for relief in the bill,
> Biden leaned forward toward into the microphone
> and whispered, "I got them $1.9 trillion in relief so
> far. They're going to be getting checks in the mail
> that are consequential this week for childcare."

> A few moments later he said, "These are really tough
> decisions senators got. I don't in any way dismiss
> what Senator Murphy says about the environment. I

119.   https://www.dailywire.com/news/biden-ripped-for-threaten-
ing-to-nuke-law-abiding-american-citizens-hes-literally-recording-
nra-ads

don't dismiss it at all. Just remind him," then hissed with eyes opened wide, "I wrote the bill on the environment."

Toward the end he said, "And guess what? Remember, you're asking me — and I'm not being critical of you all, I really mean this, those are legitimate questions you're asking me, asking me, 'Well, you know, guess what? Employers can't find workers.'" He leaned forward into the microphone again with wide eyes and whispered, "I said, 'Yeah. Pay them more.' This is an employees', employees bargaining chip now. What's happening?" [120]

We are only six months into his first term, and it is starting to get really embarrassing for the Americans who actually did vote for Joe Biden.

JUNE 27 – A BROKEN CLOCK IS RIGHT TWICE PER DAY

In retaliation for drone attacks against U.S. personnel and facilities in Iraq, Biden ordered his second attack with air strikes against Iran-backed militias in Syria.

"Specifically, the U.S. strikes targeted operational and weapons storage facilities at two locations in Syria and one location in Iraq, both of which lie close to the border between those countries," said Pentagon Press Secretary John Kirby. "Several Iran-

---

120.   https://www.dailywire.com/news/creepy-joe-trends-after-biden-keeps-whispering-at-press-conference

backed militia groups, including Kata'ib Hezbollah and Kata'ib Sayyid al-Shuhada, used these facilities."

F-15s and F-16s carried out the attacks and all pilots returned safely. Navy Cmdr. Jessica McNulty said, "Their elimination will disrupt and degrade the operational capacity of the militia groups and deter additional attacks."

Biden ordered a similar retaliatory attack back in February, when a rocket attack on our base in Northern Iraq resulted in the death of a contractor and wounded our troops. [121]

JUNE 30 – A POROUS BORDER

Border security is not about being mean to people who want a better life in America, it's about protecting Americans from criminals, terrorists, drug, and human-traffickers.

Biden's refusal to enforce immigration law resulted in a 50% rise in Fentanyl deaths, according to a Texas Sheriff. This illegal drug is smuggled across the Mexican border. Tarrant County Sheriff Bill E. Waybourn told former President Donald Trump, "We're seeing a 50% increase in deadly overdoses this year... In fact, in the first quarter of 21, it was three times the amount it was last year with fentanyl overdoses."

---

121.   https://www.usatoday.com/story/news/politics/2021/06/27/biden-orders-airstrikes-syria-iraq-iranian-backed-militias/5367769001/

"We know that the cartel, the Mexican drug cartel is responsible for where it's going and it's going all over the country," said Waybourn. "I'm in Fort Worth, but it's happening, and I'd be remiss to say, it's on every sheriff and every chief and every Director of Public Safety's radar, this business of fentanyl and the deadliness and the thread it is to us as it continues to grow."

Sheriff Waybourn confirmed that the fentanyl is coming from China and entering the U.S. through our "porous borders."

Are you listening to this Mr. Biden? America needs you to step up to the plate and show whose team you are on. [122]

122.   https://www.breitbart.com/border/2021/06/30/porous-border-causes-50-percent-spike-in-fentanyl-overdoses-texas-sheriff-tells-trump/

CHAPTER 7

JULY 2021:
UNDERMINING THE CONSTITUTION

JULY 2 – SIXTEEN CENTS = NO SENSE

In an economy burdened by high levels of inflation, where everything from housing costs to gasoline are so much more expensive than they were last year, Biden's White House account bragged on Twitter that Americans could buy an Independence Day barbecue for 16 cents cheaper than last year.

> "Planning a cookout this year? Ketchup on the news. According to the Farm Bureau, the cost of a 4th of July BBQ is down from last year. It's a fact you must-hear(d). Hot dog, the Biden economic plan is working. And that's something we can all relish."[123]

Wow. Maybe wherever you're living, 16 cents is a lot, but in my couch, I have more change.

He was criticized by liberals and conservatives alike. Leftist Ed Oswald: "What in fresh hell is this? Housing costs are up by double digits, used cars are literally appreciating on dealer's lots, and you're talking about a BBQ? ...gross. Might as well forget about everything else that's way more expensive?"

---

123.   https://twitter.com/i/web/status/1410709115333234691

Dan Price, CEO of Gravity Payments: "16 cents? Home prices are going up 24% annually right now. The median home goes up 16 cents every 1.3 seconds right now."

Rep. Burgess Owens (R-UT) said: "With an unprecedented humanitarian crisis at our border, soaring gas prices, and more out of control spending that will cripple our future generations, the Biden Administration is bragging about saving us $0.04 on sliced cheese." [124]

JULY 3 — NO SUCH THING AS AN AMERICAN

The President of the United States denies the possibility of defining America or what an American is by definition. He did this at a naturalization ceremony, where non-Americans became Americans.

> "I've often said that America is the only nation in the world founded on an idea," Biden said. "Every other nation in the world is founded on the basis of either that — geography or ethnicity or religion. You can define every — almost everyone else based on those characteristics, but you can't define America. I defy you to tell me what constitutes an American. You can't do it. We're an incredibly diverse democracy."

Is he saying we cannot define what fundamentally being an American means? It's no wonder he lets non-Americans flood our borders every day.

124.   https://www.dailywire.com/news/biden-ripped-for-bragging-about-saving-americans-16-cents-lunacy-and-divorced-from-reality

To give him the benefit of the doubt, I think he is trying to say that while we are from diverse backgrounds we are unified around the idea of freedom. The problem is that Democrats believe big government is the answer, not the free market or individual liberty.

Any way you look at it, his statement makes no sense and is offensive to everyone. [125]

JULY 4 – INDEPENDENCE FROM COVID-19 = DEPENDENCE ON BIG GOVERNMENT

At the White House Fourth of July party, Biden announces that we are close to "declaring independence" from COVID-19 pandemic.

> "The best defense against these variants is to get vaccinated. My fellow Americans, it's the most patriotic thing you can do. So please, if you haven't gotten vaccinated, do it now. For yourselves, for your loved ones, for your community," he said.

To be fair, Biden did pay homage to our nation's history and to the service and sacrifice of our military. However, COVID-19 was the overall theme as usual. For Democrats, COVID-19 is a hammer and everything else is a nail.

That's because a crisis is a terrible thing to waste. [126]

125.   https://www.dailywire.com/news/biden-you-cant-define-america-i-defy-you-to-tell-me-what-constitutes-an-american-you-cant-do-it

126.   https://www.usatoday.com/story/news/politics/2021/07/04/

JULY 6 – GIVING THE TALIBAN A WIN

As the withdrawal date Biden set nears, the U.S. military confirms it has pulled out of Bagram Airfield, its largest airfield in Afghanistan. However, they did not notify the base's new Afghan commander –– who found out 2 hours after our troops left.

JULY 8 – BIDEN'S BIGGEST MISTAKE TO DATE

Biden announces that the official end of the war in Afghanistan will be August 31. He also said that the twenty-year war was "unwinnable" and that when our troops came home, he would not give them or the nation the satisfaction of saying, "mission accomplished."

> To those calling for the U.S. to extend the military operation, Biden said "How many more, how many more thousands of American daughters and sons are you willing to risk? I will not send another generation of Americans to war in Afghanistan, with no reasonable expectation of achieving a different outcome."

Robert Gates, who served as Secretary of Defense under both George W. Bush and Barrack Obama, disagrees with Joe Biden. He said in a 60 minutes interview that he would tell all those who served in the Afghan War, "mission accomplished."

july-4th-party-biden-celebrate-covid-progress-mark-its-toll/7861510002/

"Do I trust the Taliban? No," Biden said. "But I trust the capacity of the Afghan military, who is better trained, better equipped and more competent in terms of conducting war."

Boy did he get that wrong. The Afghan military folded like a house of cards. Was it any wonder, when their allies disappeared literally overnight?

Gates also said that the Afghan military was burdened by logistics and heavy equipment when compared to the light and nimble Taliban.

President Trump had already negotiated a deal with the Taliban and set a goal of withdrawing from Afghanistan by May 2021.[127]

While I applaud the desire to end hostilities, the Biden Administration did not plan the withdrawal well –– or seemingly at all. The execution of the withdrawal was so detrimental that at the time of the writing of this book in 2022, there are still Americans and American-loving Afghan allies trapped in a regime hell-bent on finding, torturing, and executing them.[128]

Thank God for many veterans and associates who are equally hell-bent on not leaving one behind, putting their

127.   https://www.theatlantic.com/magazine/archive/2022/03/biden-afghanistan-exit-american-allies-abandoned/621307/

128.   https://www.militarytimes.com/opinion/commentary/2022/01/23/veterans-helping-afghan-veterans-allies-after-withdrawal/

livelihoods, reputations–– and in many cases their lives––
on the line to rectify the lack of planning from the Biden
Administration.

The Biden Administration failed miserably at getting our
allies and equipment out safely. Even military contract K9
units were left caged without food or water on the tarmac.[129]
The results of Biden's biggest mistake are still ongoing, and
heart-wrenching.[130] [131] [132] [133]

In one BBC story, it was reported that at least 27 children
had died within 3 days.[134] Entire families wiped out –– or
worse, underage daughters kept alive and passed around ––
simply because one member had been employed by the US
military.[135]

Robert Gates went on record to say that Joe Biden has been
"wrong on nearly every major foreign policy and national
security issue over the past four decades."[136]

129.   https://www.americanhumane.org/press-release/amer-
ican-humane-condemns-death-sentence-delivered-to-con-
tract-working-dogs-left-behind-in-kabul-afghanistan/
130.   https://www.cnn.com/2021/07/22/asia/afghanistan-interpret-
ers-taliban-reprisals-intl-hnk/index.html
131.   https://www.aljazeera.com/features/2021/6/13/be-
trayed-the-afghan-interpreters-abandoned-by-the
132.   https://www.cnn.com/2021/08/15/asia/afghanistan-interpret-
ers-us-visa-taliban-cmd-intl/index.html
133.   https://www.nytimes.com/2021/10/16/world/asia/afghani-
stan-girl-burn-evacuation-military.html
134.   https://www.bbc.com/news/world-asia-58142983
135.   https://twitter.com/jtlonsdale/status/1427392532519038978
136.   https://apnews.com/article/joe-biden-afghanistan-govern-
ment-and-politics-86f939c746c7bc56bb9f11f095a95366

JULY 15 – U.S.-GERMAN RELATIONS

Biden hosts German chancellor Angela Merkel at the White House for a bilateral meeting and press conference. Abroad, Merkel is admired by the Left. But at home, she's considered a centrist who was formerly conservative.

She's certainly very adept at political maneuvering, keeping one step behind but eventually accepting the social and cultural changes in Germany.

Merkel asked Biden if the U.S. would lift the travel ban put in place in March 2020 against Europeans entering the United States. Biden refused to answer but promised he would respond soon.

Likewise, Biden didn't get support for his opposition to the Nord Stream 2 pipeline between Russia and Germany. The pipeline will have adverse economic impact on Ukraine and is opposed by Republicans and Democrats alike.

Senator Marco Rubio (R-Fla.) insists there is bipartisan support in Congress for preventing the pipeline's completion.

In a letter written to Biden, Rubio criticized the administration's decision to waive sanctions against the company constructing the pipeline, saying it "will only endanger our democratic allies in East and Central Europe and embolden Russian President Vladimir Putin in his aggression." [137]

JULY 19 – PUSHING THE VACCINE ON JORDAN

Biden hosts His Majesty King Abdullah II of Jordan at the White House for a joint press conference. In addition to committing his unwavering support of Jordan he applauded their role in stabilizing the Middle East.

True to his anti-Israel philosophy, however, Biden also expressed his strong support for a two-state solution to the Israeli-Palestinian conflict and respect for Jordan's special role as custodian of Muslim holy places in Jerusalem.

Biden announced the delivery of 500,000 vaccines to Jordan and pushed for the same urgency to international vaccination efforts that we have demonstrated at home. [138]

JULY 20 – BIDEN ANGERS CHINA MORE THAN TRUMP

The Biden Administration angers Chinese officials by accusing them of cyberespionage and hacking.

With a broad array of allies from the European Union and members of NATO, the U.S. is criticizing China harder with

---

137.   https://www.politico.com/news/2021/07/15/biden-fare-well-angela-merkel-499790
138.   https://www.whitehouse.gov/briefing-room/statements-re-leases/2021/07/19/readout-of-President-joseph-r-biden-jr-meeting-with-king-abdullah-ii-of-jordan/

sanctions than Trump did. The Chinese Ministry of Foreign Affairs claims the accusations are "made up out of thin air."

Neither side wants a new Cold War. "The United States has declared its comeback, but the world has changed," Le Yucheng, a vice minister of foreign affairs. Relations between the two countries have deteriorated even worse under Biden. [139]

As a Communist nation, it comes as no surprise that China has a dark history of human rights violations. I was able to visit many Christians all over China—in Hong Kong and throughout the mainland—back in 2011. I was humbled by the sheer size and scale of the glimmering cities of Shanghai and Beijing.

But even more humbling and inspiring was the passion that these Christians demonstrated for their faith, many of whom had been imprisoned for much of their lives because of it. May we all be so fearless and bold!

It is important to note that China is actively practicing slavery[140] and genocide against the Uyghur Muslim minority in the Xinjiang province, even while the world's eyes are upon Beijing for the Olympics![141]

---

139.   https://www.nytimes.com/2021/07/20/world/asia/china-biden.html

140.   https://www.vox.com/the-goods/2018/10/10/17953106/walmart-prison-note-china-factory

141.   https://www.cbsnews.com/news/china-uyghurs-genocide-beijing-olympics-2022/

And we cannot fail to mention the continued abhorrent practice of forced family planning even on dangerously-late term pregnancies,[142] to the point that the State requires women to report their cycle in order to find evidence of government-banned pregnancy.[143]

JULY 22 – BIDEN UNDERMINES THE SECOND AMENDMENT

During a CNN town hall, Joe Biden proudly states he would like to ban the sale of handguns and rifles to law-abiding American citizens.

> "The idea you need a weapon that can have the ability to fire 20, 30, 40, 50, 120 shots from that weapon, whether it's a, whether it's a 9mm pistol or whether it's a rifle, is ridiculous. I'm continuing to push to eliminate the sale of those things, but I'm not likely to get that done in the near term," Biden proclaimed.

Perhaps Mr. Biden needs a history lesson as to why the Second Amendment was added to the Constitution in the first place. Our founders understood that the biggest threat to our freedom was a government run by tyrants. [144]

Their concerns in their own words speak for themselves:

142.   https://www.npr.org/2007/04/23/9766870/cases-of-forced-abortions-surface-in-china
143.   https://www.theatlantic.com/international/archive/2012/03/what-chinas-talking-about-today-a-state-exam-asks-about-menstruation/254854/
144.   https://www.dailywire.com/news/breaking-biden-indicates-he-wants-to-ban-the-sale-of-handguns

"A free people ought not only to be armed, but disciplined..." - George Washington, First Annual Address, to both House of Congress, January 8, 1790

"No free man shall ever be debarred the use of arms." - Thomas Jefferson, Virginia Constitution, Draft 1, 1776

"I prefer dangerous freedom over peaceful slavery."- Thomas Jefferson, letter to James Madison, January 30, 1787

"What country can preserve its liberties if their rulers are not warned from time to time that their people preserve the spirit of resistance. Let them take arms." - Thomas Jefferson, letter to William Stephens Smith, son-in-law of John Adams, December 20, 1787

"The laws that forbid the carrying of arms are laws of such a nature. They disarm only those who are neither inclined nor determined to commit crimes.... Such laws make things worse for the assaulted and better for the assailants; they serve rather to encourage than to prevent homicides, for an unarmed man may be attacked with greater confidence than an armed man." - Thomas Jefferson, Commonplace Book (quoting 18th century criminologist Cesare Beccaria), 1774-1776

"A strong body makes the mind strong. As to the species of exercises, I advise the gun. While this gives moderate exercise to the body, it gives boldness, enterprise and independence to the mind. Games played with the ball, and others of that nature, are too violent for the body and stamp no character on the mind. Let your gun therefore be your constant companion of your walks." - Thomas Jefferson, letter to Peter Carr, August 19, 1785

"The Constitution of most of our states (and of the United States) assert that all power is inherent in the people; that they may exercise it by themselves; that it is their right and duty to be at all times armed."- Thomas Jefferson, letter to John Cartwright, 5 June 1824

"They that can give up essential liberty to obtain a little temporary safety deserve neither liberty nor safety."- Benjamin Franklin, Historical Review of Pennsylvania, 1759

"To disarm the people...[i]s the most effectual way to enslave them." - George Mason, referencing advice given to the British Parliament by Pennsylvania governor Sir William Keith, The Debates in the Several State Conventions on the Adoption of the Federal Constitution, June 14, 1788

"I ask who are the militia? They consist now of the whole people, except a few public officers." - George Mason, Address to the Virginia Ratifying Convention, June 4, 1788

"Before a standing army can rule, the people must be disarmed, as they are in almost every country in Europe. The supreme power in America cannot enforce unjust laws by the sword; because the whole body of the people are armed and constitute a force superior to any band of regular troops." - Noah Webster, An Examination of the Leading Principles of the Federal Constitution, October 10, 1787

"Besides the advantage of being armed, which the Americans possess over the people of almost every other nation, the existence of subordinate governments, to which the people are attached, and by which the militia officers are appointed, forms a barrier against the enterprises of ambition, more insurmountable than any which a simple government of any form can admit of." - James Madison, Federalist No. 46, January 29, 1788

"The right of the people to keep and bear arms shall not be infringed. A well-regulated militia, composed of the body of the people, trained to arms, is the best and most natural defense of a free country."- James Madison, I Annals of Congress 434, June 8, 1789

"...the ultimate authority, wherever the derivative may be found, resides in the people alone..."- James Madison, Federalist No. 46, January 29, 1788

"Necessity is the plea for every infringement of human freedom. It is the argument of tyrants; it is the creed of slaves."- William Pitt (the Younger), Speech in the House of Commons, November 18, 1783

"A militia when properly formed are in fact the people themselves...and include, according to the past and general usage of the states, all men capable of bearing arms... "To preserve liberty, it is essential that the whole body of the people always possess arms, and be taught alike, especially when young, how to use them." - Richard Henry Lee, Federal Farmer No. 18, January 25, 1788

"Guard with jealous attention the public liberty. Suspect everyone who approaches that jewel. Unfortunately, nothing will preserve it but downright force. Whenever you give up that force, you are ruined.... The great object is that every man be armed. Everyone who is able might have a gun." - Patrick Henry, Speech to the Virginia Ratifying Convention, June 5, 1778

"This may be considered as the true palladium of liberty.... The right of self-defense is the first law of nature: in most governments it has been the study of rulers to confine this right within the narrowest limits possible. Wherever standing armies are kept up, and the right of the people to keep and bear arms is, under any color or pretext whatsoever, prohibited, liberty, if not already annihilated, is on the brink of destruction." - St. George Tucker, Blackstone's Commentaries on the Laws of England, 1803

"The supposed quietude of a good man allures the ruffian; while on the other hand, arms, like law, discourage and keep the invader and the plunderer in awe, and preserve order in the world as well as property. The balance of power is the scale of peace. The same balance would be preserved were all the world destitute of arms, for all would be alike; but since some will not, others dare not lay them aside. And while a single nation refuses to lay them down, it is proper that all should keep them up. Horrid mischief would ensue were one-half the world deprived of the use of them; for while avarice and ambition have a place in the heart of man, the weak will become a prey to the strong. The history of every age and nation establishes these truths, and facts need but little arguments when they prove themselves." - Thomas Paine, "Thoughts on Defensive War" in Pennsylvania Magazine, July 1775

"The Constitution shall never be construed to prevent the people of the United States who are peaceable citizens from keeping their own arms." - Samuel Adams, Massachusetts Ratifying Convention, 1788

"The right of the citizens to keep and bear arms has justly been considered, as the palladium of the liberties of a republic; since it offers a strong moral check against the usurpation and arbitrary power of rulers; and will generally, even if these are successful in the first instance, enable the people to resist and triumph over them." - Joseph Story, Commentaries on the Constitution of the United States, 1833

"What, Sir, is the use of a militia? It is to prevent the establishment of a standing army, the bane of liberty .... Whenever Governments mean to invade the rights and liberties of the people, they always attempt to destroy the militia, in order to raise an army upon their ruins." - Rep. Elbridge Gerry of Massachusetts, I Annals of Congress 750, August 17, 1789

"For it is a truth, which the experience of ages has attested, that the people are always most in danger when the means of injuring their rights are in the possession of those of whom they entertain the least suspicion." - Alexander Hamilton, Federalist No. 25, December 21, 1787

"If the representatives of the people betray their constituents, there is then no resource left but in the exertion of that original right of self-defense which is paramount to all positive forms of government, and which against the usurpations of the national rulers, may be exerted with infinitely better prospect of success than against those of the rulers of an individual state. In a single state, if the persons entrusted with supreme power become usurpers, the different parcels, subdivisions, or districts of which it consists, having no distinct government in each, can take no regular measures for defense. The citizens must rush tumultuously to arms, without concert, without system, without resource; except in their courage and despair." - Alexander Hamilton, Federalist No. 28

"[I]f circumstances should at any time oblige the government to form an army of any magnitude that army can never be formidable to the liberties of the people while there is a large body of citizens, little, if at all, inferior to them in discipline and the use of arms, who stand ready to defend their own rights and those of their fellow-citizens. This appears to me the only substitute that can be devised for a standing army, and the best possible security against it, if it should exist." - Alexander Hamilton, Federalist No. 28, January 10, 1788

"As civil rulers, not having their duty to the people before them, may attempt to tyrannize, and as the military forces which must be occasionally raised to defend our country, might pervert their power to the injury of their fellow citizens, the people are confirmed by the article in their right to keep and bear their private arms." - Tench Coxe, Philadelphia Federal Gazette, June 18, 1789

As you can see, the original intent of the founding fathers and their interpretation of the Second Amendment is crystal clear. Democrats are threatened by original intent because it threatens what they believe to be their supreme power over their "subjects."

It is interesting to note that at the time of the Revolution of the Colonies against the Crown, over 40% were of Scots-Irish descent.

In his book, *Born Fighting: How the Scots-Irish Shaped America*, Jim Webb provides both a distinguished work of cultural history and a human drama that speaks straight to the heart of historic and even contemporary America.

It doesn't take much research to be shocked and horrified at the tragedies and downright acts of terrorism against the Scots-Irish at the hands of their English overlords during the 17th and 18th centuries.[145] [146]

From the banning of the bagpipes, to the outlawing of fabric pinned at the shoulder, to the theft of personal property, to the ban of all weapons, to massacres and mass executions without due process, the Scots-Irish who made up such a large percentage of the Colonial Army in 1775 would have been a mere 30 years (give or take) from experiencing what government overreach felt like.

They not only fought tooth and nail to win the War, they poured their hopes and hearts into our Constitution. They knew, many first-hand, that to preserve this more perfect Union, establish Justice, insure domestic Tranquility, provide for the common defense, promote the general Welfare, and secure the blessings of Liberty for themselves and for their posterity required the Amendments they penned.

The author of my foreword, Joe Visconti, points out that Joe Biden in coordination with leaders of the Democrat

145.   https://www.thenational.scot/news/17218815.after-math-culloden-end-jacobites/
146.   https://www.politico.eu/article/6-times-the-irish-learned-not-to-trust-london-history-brexit/

Party, elements of the United States Government, the Intelligence community, the Mainstream Media, Big Tech, Big Pharma, Wall Street, Big oil, Academia and Hollywood are attempting to rewrite this preamble to read:

We the Permanent Establishment of the United States, in order to form a more defective Union, establish injustice, insure domestic turmoil, provide for common harm, promote general Adversity, and secure the Curses of Captivity to the unwashed masses and their Posterity, do ordain and establish this Plutocracy for the United States of America.

After all, Biden can't even remember the preamble from the Declaration of Independence. [147]

JULY 23 – PLUMMETING APPROVAL RATING

Biden's approval rating falls from 56% in June to 50% in July. 90% of Democrats and only 12% of Republicans approve of his Presidency. Affecting his rating are concerns about rising inflation, the increasing numbers of migrants crossing our southern border illegally, and the Delta variant of the coronavirus which even infects vaccinated Americans.

How much further will it fall? [148]

---

147.   https://conservative-daily.com/election/omg-joe-biden-forgot-preamble-to-the-declaration-of-independence
148.   https://www.breitbart.com/politics/2021/07/23/gallup-joe-biden-registers-lowest-approval-rating-of-his-presidency/

JULY 26 – ATTACKING FEMALE REPORTERS

Biden snapped and cut off NBC's Kelly O'Donnell, a female reporter, before she could finish her question about the VA vaccine mandate:

> "Mr. President, Veterans Affairs is going to have a mandate for its healthcare–"

Biden was apparently irritated that the question had nothing to do with his recent meeting with Iraqi Prime Minister Mustafa Al-Kadhimi, so he rudely interrupted her with this harsh criticism,

> "You are such a pain in the neck, but I'm going to answer your question because we've known each other so long. It has nothing to do with Iraq. Yes, Veteran Affairs is going to, in fact, require that all doctors working in their facilities are gonna have to be vaccinated."

CNN political commentator Scott Jennings responded to the incident by writing on Twitter: "Verbally abusive and dismissive of a female journalist. Keeps happening over and over. Why?"

Earlier this year Biden joked about running over a female reporter while test driving a new Ford truck. Why aren't more people on the Left concerned about this mistreatment of women?

Many are calling for the President to undergo a cognitive exam to determine his fitness for office. [149]

JULY 29 – MORE LOCKDOWNS

The Biden Administration says that it will return to school lockdowns if the CDC recommends it.

> Principal Deputy Press Secretary Karine Jean-Pierre said, "This is a public health situation. This is not about politics at all. This is about saving lives. And this is what the President is all about. He wants to make sure that we are saving lives. If you look at ... the last six months, that's what he's done, every day. And you see that in the numbers. Now we're at a point where we have to double down and make it very, very clear to people that we can't, we can't let the pandemic win, we have to continue to fight."

Can you believe they are still pushing draconian lockdowns despite the rising evidence that children are suffering academic and emotional setbacks from being subjected to online distance learning? [150]

COVID is not a concern for most healthy children. With mask and vaccine mandates in place, which are supposed to protect from COVID, why are the teachers still worried? [151]

149.   https://www.dailywire.com/news/biden-snaps-at-female-re-porter-over-question-you-are-such-a-pain-in-the-neck
150.   https://reliefweb.int/report/world/covid-19-children-globally-struggling-after-lockdowns-averaging-six-months-save
151.   https://www.dailywire.com/news/breaking-biden-administra-tion-signals-it-is-willing-to-return-to-lockdowns-school-closures-if-

JULY 29 – CONFUSED ABOUT MASKS

Mr. Biden contradicts what he promised earlier in the
year when he says that vaccinated Americans should wear
masks, yet while giving the announcement at the White
House, Biden removed his mask! In fact, he broke the newly
released guidance for Washington, DC, requiring everyone
to wear masks indoors. [152]

Democrats have created so many COVID rules and flipped-
flopped on them so many times that they can't seem to keep
it all straight.

Once again, the rest of us are just shaking our heads at the
unbelievable ineptitude of government—specifically the
Biden-Harris Regime.

JULY 29 – BRIBING LOCAL GOVERNMENTS TO PUSH THE JAB

Biden asks local governments to use Federal funds to give
$100 to each person who gets vaccinated as US COVID
vaccination rates lag behind other countries, despite ample
availability.

> "Right now too many people are dying or watching
> someone they love dying. With freedom comes
> responsibility. So please exercise responsible

---

recommended-by-cdc
152.   https://www.breitbart.com/politics/2021/07/29/confused-joe-
biden-struggles-with-inconsistent-message-on-mask-mandates/

judgment. Get vaccinated for yourself, the people
you love, for your country."[153]

Yet when many Americans take his statement and exercise
their responsible judgement to decline to obtain the
vaccine, he quickly sets mandates in motion against them.

Requiring federal workers to provide proof of vaccination or
face regular testing, mask mandates and travel restrictions,
Biden demands,

> "Every Federal employee will be asked to attest to
> their vaccination status. Anyone who does not attest
> or is not vaccinated will require to mask no matter
> where they work, test one or two times per week to
> see if they've acquired COVID, socially distance, and
> generally will not be allowed to travel for work."

Wow. Sounds like the Federal government is creating a clas-
sification of second-class citizens who have fewer rights and
opportunities and they're doing it right before our eyes.

JULY 30 – JUST PLAIN GROSS

During a virtual meeting that Joe and Kamala attended
with governors about wildfires rampaging parts of the
country, Biden is handed a note by a staffer telling him he

153.
 https://www.reuters.com/world/us/biden-federal-worker-vaccina-
tion-push-affect-millions-2021-07-29/

has something on his chin. The video shows him wiping the material off his chin and appearing to put it in his mouth. [154]

I'm not sure what he should have done with the substance, or what the substance was, but putting it in my mouth would not have been my first move, especially if I was live!

Perhaps it was a drip of ice-cream?

154.   https://www.dailywire.com/news/biden-handed-embarrass-ing-note-during-meeting-gets-mocked-for-what-he-does-next

CHAPTER 8
AUGUST 2022:
THE AUGUST CURSE

Presidential Historian Jon Meacham reminds us that, "History happens in August. The beginning of World War I; Hitler amassing troops for the invasion of Poland; Truman's dropping the atomic bombs; LBJ's signing the Voting Rights Act; Nixon's resignation; Reagan's firing the air traffic controllers, the invasion of Kuwait for George H.W. Bush; Clinton's grand jury testimony and the strike against Bin Laden; Katrina. I can go on."

AUGUST 6 – BIDEN VACATIONS WHILE AFGHANISTAN UNRAVELS

Regardless of their political party, the scrutiny that a President undergoes is relentless from all sides. Every word uttered and every decision made is weighed on blogs and news networks 24/7.

The Leftwing media is much easier on Democrats, of course. Like the rest of us, Presidents need to rest to be at their best for their country. George W. Bush loved golf. Obama flew to Hawaii many times. President Trump spent ample time at his various properties. All of them were criticized for this at one time or another by both sides of the MSM.

But today, Biden begins a vacation in Wilmington, Delaware, one of many that has already been completed![155] Events that will unfold in the coming days will show that the timing of this getaway was particularly unfortunate.

On this very day the Taliban took control of its first province — the capital of Nimroz province in Afghanistan — sending terror through the many Americans and American allies trapped in Afghanistan and breaking their agreement with the U.S. government.

Big surprise.[156]

AUGUST 8 – STAY THE COURSE... ALL THE WAY TO FAILURE

After humiliating Biden, and therefore the entire United States, by capturing two Afghan cities –– Sheberghan and Zaranj –– the Administration sends B-52s to attack Taliban forces. The goal is to keep enemy forces from taking over more cities.

At this point, only 650 troops are left to defend the U.S. Embassy and the Capitol. However, 20,000 defense contractors are still left behind and attempting to prop up the faltering Afghan government.

155.   https://www.politico.com/newsletters/west-wing-play-book/2021/08/09/vacation-all-i-ever-wanted-493912
156.   https://www.nbcnews.com/news/world/taliban-over-runs-first-afghan-provincial-capital-u-s-began-withdrawal-n1276175

Biden does not adjust the timeline for an August 31st withdrawal despite indications – and warnings – that it will go very, very badly. [157]

AUGUST 11 – ANOTHER BIDEN GAFFE

Michigan Governor Gretchen Whitmer was rumored to be one of the top picks for Biden's running mate. But he got her name wrong at a White House meeting about the Democrat's $1 trillion infrastructure bill when he said, "Thank you, Jennifer, for what you've done."

According to the Detroit Free Press, Biden was returning a compliment after Whitmer had thanked him for leading the effort to get the bill passed. This is just one more example of the exhibited signs of Biden's cognitive failure.

This is not the first time she's been called Jennifer at a public event. Many confuse her with former Governor Jennifer Granholm (2003 – 2011). During his Presidency, Donald Trump referred to her as "that woman from Michigan." [158]

Biden's Wilmington getaway is interrupted by the Afghanistan crisis, and he spends a long weekend at Camp David instead, keeping out of the public eye.

---

157.   https://www.express.co.uk/news/world/1473841/joe-biden-news-US-B52s-taliban-bombed-afghanistan-sheberghan-captured
158.   https://www.foxnews.com/politics/biden-gaffe-President-calls-michigans-whitmer-jennifer-at-white-house-event-report-says

AUGUST 12 – NO MORE MASKS!

At the White House, Biden calls school administrators enforcing mask mandates 'heroes' and excoriated those who protest mask mandates.

> "To the mayors, school superintendents, educators, local leaders who are standing up to the governors politicizing mask protection for our kids – thank you," Biden said.

> "I know there are a lot of people trying to turn a public safety measure, that is children wearing masks in school so they can be safe, into a political dispute," Biden stated judgingly. This isn't about politics; this is about keeping our children safe."

Biden is referring to the protest that broke out at a Tennessee school, where an anti-mask doctor was removed from a meeting and parents chanted, "No more masks!" [159]

Children are at less risk from COVID-19, and the effectiveness of masks is questionable at best. N95 masks are much more effective compared to the bandanas and paper masks you see around, yet the government doesn't enforce N95. Why not? Because it seems to be more about control than efficacy.

---

159.   https://www.breitbart.com/politics/2021/08/12/joe-biden-thanks-heroes-forcing-mask-mandates-children/

AUGUST 16 – AMERICA'S LONGEST WAR

Biden cuts his Camp David vacation short to come back to Washington as America's longest war comes to a bloody end. Approximately 6,000 troops were sent to Kabul to ensure the safe departure of Americans and their diplomatic allies.

However, the day turned deadly as several Afghans tried to escape. They knew their world was about to change fast and for the worst. Still, the speed at which the Taliban took control and the Afghan government collapsed was shocking. Some attempted to flee by clinging to the side of a U.S. military transport jet and fell to their deaths. This tragedy was captured on video and went viral. The world was stunned.

While the events that transpired severely tarnished the reputation of the Biden Administration, Biden defended his decision to withdraw from Afghanistan! He said he stood "squarely behind" it.

"After 20 years I've learned the hard way there was never a good time to withdraw our forces," Biden said. "That's why we're still there."

"This is a damning image for the Biden Administration and underscores the magnitude of the humanitarian crisis on the ground," House Republican Leader Kevin McCarthy said. Senate Republican Leader Mitch McConnell said the events that unfolded in Afghanistan were a "shameful failure of American leadership." [160]

Later that afternoon, Biden gives a speech to the press at the White House about the botched withdrawal from Afghanistan. He explained that the original purpose of our presence in Afghanistan was to stop terrorism rather than nation building.

Biden is the fourth President to oversee the war in Afghanistan. Biden made it known that he wanted this to end on his watch, rather than pass it on to a future President.

> "The scenes we're seeing in Afghanistan, they're gut-wrenching, particularly for our veterans, our diplomats, humanitarian workers, for anyone who has spent time on the ground working to support the Afghan people. For those who have lost loved ones in Afghanistan and for Americans who have fought and served in the country — serve our country in Afghanistan — this is deeply, deeply personal," Biden said.

> "I made a commitment to the American people when I ran for President that I would bring America's military involvement in Afghanistan to an end. And while it's been hard and messy — and yes, far from perfect — I've honored that commitment."

---

160.   https://kfor.com/news/biden-to-address-nation-on-chaos-in-afghanistan/

After the speech, Biden bolted and refused to take questions from reporters. [161]

If you speak with any number of veterans of this war, you'll hear a very strongly-worded opinion of how the Biden Administration failed during the Afghanistan withdrawal fiasco.

AUGUST 18 – BIDEN LEAVES AMERICANS BEHIND

The Biden Defense Department admits they are unable to rescue Americans stranded in Afghanistan and that the Taliban are not honoring their agreement to allow Americans and Afghans with visas to leave safely. There are still 10,000 – 15,000 Americans in Afghanistan. Those trying to make it to the Kabul airport cannot get through Taliban checkpoints.

Defense Secretary Lloyd Austin did not give them much hope when he said, "We don't have the capability to go out and collect large numbers of people." The Defense Department said they "don't have the capability" to save Americans in Afghanistan who can't get to Kabul's airport, and that they will stay on the ground "until the clock runs out."

This is like admitting you're so many points behind in the game that you're wasting the final few minutes just sitting

161.   https://www.dailywire.com/news/breaking-biden-bolts-from-press-conference-on-afghanistan-refuses-to-take-questions-from-media

around waiting for the buzzer to sound before admitting you've lost. [162]

AUGUST 19 – TWENTY MYTHS, LIES, AND HALF-TRUTHS ABOUT AFGHANISTAN

Biden gives an interview with ABC's George Stephanopoulos where he gets at least 20 basic facts wrong regarding the withdrawal from Afghanistan.

It is concerning that the President of the United States is either not in possession of the facts or is trying to deceptively cast his actions in a more positive light by misrepresenting the facts. Which is it? Either way it's atrocious.

1. He claimed there was no consensus in intelligence reports that the Taliban would take control. Not true.

2. He claimed he always said there was a "real possibility" that the Taliban would seize control of Afghanistan. Not true.

3. He defended his 'withdrawal' of troops while simultaneously sending 6,000 more into harm's way. Which is it, Joe?

---

162.   https://www.dailywire.com/news/biden-admin-we-dont-have-the-capability-to-rescue-americans-trapped-in-afghanistan-taliban-not-honoring-safe-passage-agreement

4. He claimed we had built an Afghan army of 300,000 troops, which is a highly inflated number.

5. He claimed the timeline for withdrawal was firm, but he himself had changed it many times.

6. He claims his military advisors did not warn against his withdrawal timeline, yet evidence abounds that his Generals did advise him to keep troops in the region.

7. He claims he took precautions by sending 6,000 troops to Afghanistan, but the Afghan government was already in the process of collapsing by that point.

8. Biden claimed nobody was getting killed around the Kabul airport when there had already been 12 confirmed deaths.

9. Biden claims the tragedy of people falling off a C-17 was "4-5 days ago," but it had happened just 3 days prior.

10. Biden stumbles over basic details of his son's military service. Perhaps because he was discharged for failing a drug test?[163]

11. Biden blows off a serious question about America's reputation in Asia and around the world.

---

163.   https://www.reuters.com/article/uk-fact-check-hunter-biden-not-dishonora-idUSKBN26M6QI

12. Biden makes the misleading statement that the Taliban was taking territory "all throughout the country" before Trump's May 1st deadline.

13. Biden claims he made 'No' mistakes and could not have handled the exit from Afghanistan any better. Many of our active-duty military and many of our veterans disagree with you, Joe.

14. Biden says the Taliban is cooperating, but other times says he does not trust them. Perhaps because they were not keeping their promises?

15. Biden claims the Taliban is granting "safe passage" to Americans. Not true.

16. Biden makes a promise to evacuate Afghan women and girls if they get to the airport in Kabul, but his Administration has already stated he cannot deliver on this promise.

17. Biden waffles on withdrawing the remaining American troops in Kabul after the August 31 deadline, but ultimately says he will miss the deadline.

18. Biden claims America does not have military troops in Syria. We have approximately 900.

19. Joe Biden claims the Taliban will not be the same as they were in 2001. True. But this is only because they are now more powerful and control more territory!

20. Biden contradicts his earlier statements that the mission in Afghanistan was accomplished and that nation-building "never made any sense to me." When he was a Senator in 2002 and 2003, he supported nation-building in Afghanistan. [164]

AUGUST 23 — BIG PHARMA DISTRACTION

Attempting to distract the country away from the debacle in Afghanistan, Biden delivered a speech about the FDA giving full approval to Pfizer's vaccine, urging Americans to get vaccinated.

At the end, a reporter asked Biden, "Do you know how many Americans are left in Afghanistan sir?" Biden walked away and did not respond. It doesn't appear that Biden will be able to get all Americans out of Afghanistan by the August 31 deadline.

When questioned by reporters about the Administration's promise to get more Americans out of the country, Pentagon spokesman John Kirby answered vaguely, "I'm just going to leave it at several thousand."

National Security Advisor Jake Sullivan said, "The President believes we are making substantial progress." [165]

164.   https://www.breitbart.com/politics/2021/08/19/coming-un-glued-20-mistakes-joe-biden-made-bumbling-afghanistan-inter-view/
165.   https://www.breitbart.com/politics/2021/08/23/joe-biden-walks-away-questions-thousands-americans-still-stranded-afghan-istan/

AUGUST 24 – LACK OF CONFIDENCE IN THE BIDEN ADMINISTRATION

According to a Gallup poll, only 23 percent of Americans are satisfied with "the way things are going." This is the lowest point since Biden took office on January 20th and coincides with his overall approval rating which dropped from 50% to 44% overnight. [166]

AUGUST 24 – SMACKED DOWN BY THE HIGHEST COURT

The Supreme Court rules that Biden must reinstate Trump's "Remain in Mexico" doctrine. This means that asylum seekers must remain in Mexico rather than in the US while their case is pending.

Those on the Left are concerned that Mexico is too dangerous and that asylum seekers are often raped, kidnapped, or killed while waiting. As a Christian and a compassionate Conservative, I share this concern, and it weighs heavy on me. But how do we address this challenge without weakening America in the process?

This is a moral question that we need to address from a Biblical perspective, not with a State-run savior complex. [167]

166. https://www.breitbart.com/politics/2021/08/24/u-s-satisfaction-drops-bidens-presidency/
167. https://www.politico.com/news/2021/08/24/trump-mexico-border-supreme-court-506833

AUGUST 26 – DON'T TALK TO STRANGERS

Naturally, Biden is given a list of pre-picked reporters to call on at a press conference about the disastrous withdrawal from Afghanistan. "Ladies and gentlemen, they gave me a list here. The first person I was instructed to call on was Kelly O'Donnell of NBC," admitted Biden.

Trump's White House Press Secretary, Kayleigh McEnany, said nothing like this ever happened during the Trump presidency. Criticizing the Biden Administration on Twitter she said, "As White House Press Secretary, I NEVER instructed President Trump to call on a pre-determined list of reporters. President Trump could make decisions for himself, speak directly to the American people, and secure peace through strength..." [168]

If only Biden's handlers felt the same about him. It would seem any reporter should be able to ask any question of the President of the United States of America in order to do their duty in journalistic reporting to the American people for the sake of transparency in government.

It seems clear that the Biden-Harris Administration does not desire transparency in government.

---

168. https://www.dailywire.com/news/biden-admits-to-being-instructed-which-reporters-to-call-on-trump-press-sec-condemns

AUGUST 27 – CHALLENGING THE TRANSGENDER MANDATE

Over 3,000 pediatricians and medical professionals sue the Biden Administration, *American College of Pediatricians v. Becerra,* for a mandate that doctors must give hormones and surgery to transgender individuals even if they have medical or other objections.

The suit was filed with the U.S. District Court for the Eastern District of Tennessee at Chattanooga. Alliance Defending Freedom (ADF) is representing more than 3,000 physicians and health care professionals. In a press release about the suit, ADF stated,

> "The American College of Pediatricians, the Catholic Medical Association, and an OB-GYN doctor who specializes in caring for adolescents filed suit in federal court to challenge a Biden Administration mandate requiring doctors to perform gender transition procedures on any patient, including a child, if the procedure violates a doctor's medical judgment or religious beliefs."

> "The U.S. Department of Health and Human Services reinterpreted non-discrimination on the basis of sex in the Affordable Care Act to include gender identity and thus require gender transition interventions, services, surgeries, and drugs on demand, even for children, no matter a doctor's medical judgment, religious beliefs, or conscientious objection." [169]

---

169.   https://www.dailywire.com/news/3000-plus-pediatri-

The Left, with an ever-changing moral compass, continues to push society closer to the cliff each day. What is their end game?

I believe they are systematically destroying individual liberty, the family unit, and relevance of the Church to give ultimate power to the State. It's already happening, and we must turn the tide before it's too late.

AUGUST 27 – RACIAL GAFFES CONTINUE

In another racial gaffe, Biden calls a Black Senior Adviser 'boy' at a FEMA briefing after Hurricane Ida slammed Louisiana. "I'm here with my senior adviser and boy who knows Louisiana very, very well and New Orleans, Cedric Richmond," Biden said.

Using the term "boy" when speaking of a Black man is considered extremely derogatory.

President Trump was often unfairly accused of racism, but the mainstream media has given Biden a pass on far worse behavior.

GOP National Spokesperson Paris Dennard tweeted, "Cedric Richmond is a 47-year-old man. While Ja'Ron Smith was 38 years old when he was in a similar role for President Trump, I can assure he was not called a "boy" by

President Trump. Joe Biden just continues to insult Black men openly and in public because he doesn't care."[170]

AUGUST 30 – BIDEN HANDS AFGHANISTAN BACK TO THE TALIBAN

Today marks the official end of the war in Afghanistan, including any efforts to evacuate Americans, vulnerable Afghan allies, and third-party nationals.

> General Kenneth F. McKenzie, Jr., commander of U.S. Central Command, opened a press briefing with this statement, "I'm here to announce the completion of our withdrawal from Afghanistan and the end of the military mission to evacuate American citizens, third-country nationals and vulnerable Afghans. The last C-17 lifted off from Hamid Karzai International Airport this afternoon at 3:29 p.m. East Coast time and the last manned aircraft is now clearing the airspace above Afghanistan. We will soon release a photo of the last C-17 departing Afghanistan with Major General Chris Donahue and the U.S. ambassador to Afghanistan, Ross Wilson, aboard."[171]

Biden vowed to remain in Afghanistan until all Americans who wished to leave were out, promising, "If there are

170.   https://www.foxnews.com/politics/biden-calls-Black-adviser-boy
171.   https://www.defense.gov/News/Transcripts/Transcript/Article/2759183/pentagon-press-secretary-john-f-kirby-and-general-kenneth-f-mckenzie-jr-hold-a/

American citizens left, we're going to stay until we get them all out."

Foreign Policy Magazine reports that the State Department believed as many as 14,000 Americans were still in the country trying to leave. [172] The Administration continually claimed there are only between 100 - 200 Americans remaining who want to leave.

On Aug. 30, Secretary of State Antony Blinken said: "We believe there are still a small number of Americans — under 200 and likely closer to 100 — who remain in Afghanistan and want to leave." Senator Jim Inhofe (R-Oklahoma) stated last month: "The Administration's number of US citizens left in Afghanistan keeps changing... It's very confusing." [173]

He did not keep this promise. At the writing of this book in 2022, teams of veterans are still actively engaged in aiding and attempting to evacuate hundreds still in hiding and fearing for their lives.

172.   https://foreignpolicy.com/2021/11/03/state-department-afghanistan-us-residents/
173.   https://nypost.com/2021/11/13/team-bidens-neverending-lies-about-those-left-in-afghanistan/

CHAPTER 9

SEPTEMBER 2021:
AMERICANS CHANT "F--K JOE BIDEN"

SEPTEMBER 3-4 – "FJB" CHANTS SWEEP THE NATION

For the past four weeks, crowds at college football games and at other various sporting events across the nation erupt in chants of "F—k Joe Biden!" Both participation and frequency are intensifying this weekend, and the Left cannot escape it. The chant could even be heard from the crowd at the Evander Holyfield vs. Vítor Vieira Belfort fight!

Clearly this is a result of the frustration over Biden's disastrous handling of the Afghanistan crisis, the pandemic, the economy, and practically every other domestic and international issue imaginable. [174]

SEPTEMBER 6 – SAY IT AIN'T SO, JOE

Rick Clay, the head of a private rescue organization called PlanB, claims that the Biden Administration is blocking attempts to rescue Americans and visa holders stuck in Afghanistan. If this sounds hard to believe, consider the fact that these private rescue missions underscore the failure of the Biden Administration to get Americans out in the first place.

---

174.   https://www.breitbart.com/sports/2021/09/26/watch-fck-joe-biden-chant-rings-out-at-wisconsin-notre-dame-game/

According to Fox News, the State Department is the only thing preventing the flights he's organizing from leaving Afghanistan. "Two other American individuals separately involved in evacuation efforts, whom Fox News is not naming to avoid jeopardizing ongoing rescue efforts, similarly said that the State Department is the sole entity preventing their charter flights from leaving Afghanistan."

One of the individuals that Fox News spoke to said that "all it takes is a F--king phone call" to fix the problem and that it was unacceptable to be "negotiating with American lives."

"If one life is lost as a result of this, the blood is on the White House's hands. The blood is on their hands," that individual said. "It is not the Taliban that is holding this up – as much as it sickens me to say that – it is the United States government."

Rep. Dan Crenshaw (R-TX) tweeted, "America: right now there is a private effort to get a plane of US citizens and allies out of Afghanistan. They need @SecBlinken to help get clearance to land in a nearby country.

Biden's State Department is refusing to actively assist. Their response: 'just tell them to ask.'"[175]

---

175.   https://www.dailywire.com/news/breaking-biden-ad-min-blocking-private-flights-from-evacuating-americans-out-of-af-ghanistan-report

SEPTEMBER 9 – BIDEN FORCES MEDICAL PROCEDURES ON AMERICANS

Breaking another of his promises, Biden announces mandate for companies with over 100 employees to require vaccinations or weekly testing.

White House Press Secretary Jen Psaki gave a preview of the plan, "There are –– there are six new –– there are six steps the President is announcing. There will be new components, as I noted, and you noted. Some of that will be related to access to testing. Some will be related to mandates. Some will be related to how we ensure kids are protected in schools," Psaki continued.

"And we'll have more –– we'll preview more tomorrow as all the pieces are finalized. But there will be new components that, sure, will of course impact people across the country. But we're also all working together to get the virus under control, to return to our normal lives. And I know many people, I'm sure, are looking forward to hearing what the President has to say."

The mandate will be "enacted through a forthcoming rule from the Occupational Safety and Health Administration that carries penalties of $14,000 per violation, an Administration official said," per the Associated Press.

While some parts of the federal government have already mandated vaccines for employees, including U.S. military servicemen, this is the first time Biden is coming after private businesses and American citizens. [176]

And OSHA is notoriously short-staffed and leaderless.[177] How will they enforce such government overreach?

SEPTEMBER 9 – RNC SUES BIDEN

The RNC announces plans to sue Biden Administration over his unconstitutional vaccine mandate. After he was elected, Biden promised, "I don't think it should be mandatory. I wouldn't demand it be mandatory."

Just before he found out the RNC was going to sue his Administration, Biden said, "This is not about freedom or personal choice. ... It's about protecting yourself and those around you" as his justification for mandating vaccines.

RNC Chairwoman, Ronna McDaniel stated, "Joe Biden told Americans when he was elected that he would not impose vaccine mandates. He lied. Now small businesses, workers, and families across the country will pay the price. Like many Americans, I am pro-vaccine and anti-mandate," she clarified. "Many small businesses and workers do not have the money or legal resources to fight Biden's unconstitutional actions and authoritarian decrees." [178]

176.   https://www.dailywire.com/news/breaking-biden-to-force-private-companies-to-mandate-vaccinations-weekly-covid-tests-report
177.   https://www.ishn.com/articles/110863-neglect-leaves-osha-short-staffed-and-leaderless
178.   https://www.breitbart.com/politics/2021/09/09/

SEPTEMBER 9 – SIC SEMPER TYRANNIS

In a negative reaction to the announcement of the vaccine mandate, social media erupts with the rallying cry: "We will not comply."

> "Biden does not have the power to do what he is doing. He is not a king. He is a politician, and this is still the United States of America. He must be defied. All Americans who care about their freedom should tell this decaying old tyrant to go to hell." — Matt Walsh (@MattWalshBlog)

Donald Trump Jr. tweeted, "Where's all the oppressive totalitarian dictator talk???" questioned Donald Trump Jr. "We heard it for 5 years for everything and anything Trump said but the press and the left is strangely silent when there's actually totalitarianism happening???"

Daily Wire co-founder and CEO Jeremy Boreing tweeted, "The Daily Wire has well over 100 employees. We will not enforce Joe Biden's unconstitutional and tyrannical vaccine mandate," Boreing wrote. "We will use every tool at our disposal, including legal action, to resist this overreach. More to come."

The Blaze CEO, Tyler Cardon, echoed. "Yeah, I sure as s*** won't be enforcing a vaccine mandate."

---

rnc-sue-biden-admin-unconstitutional-vaccinate-mandate/

Rep. Thomas Massie (R-KY) called the dictate "absolutely unconstitutional."

Mike Dunleavy, Governor of Alaska, tweeted, "This is ridiculous and unenforceable. If there was ever a case for the 25th Amendment..." [179]

SEPTEMBER 10 – CONCERNS OVER BIDEN'S LEADERSHIP SWELL

A CNN poll reveals only 2% of Americans think that America is doing "very well" under Biden. For comparison, a similar poll in January before President Trump left office showed 21% of Americans thought America was doing very well. 69% of respondents thought that America was doing badly or very badly.

Let's compare what people were worried about during President Trump's last year (2020) vs. Biden's first year (2021). 58% were worried about the economy in 2020, up to 77% in 2021. 37% were worried about crime in 2020, up to 57% in 2021. Concern over the coronavirus pandemic is up from 60% in 2020 to 70% in 2021. When ranking the concerns of the poll respondents, Coronavirus was first at 36%, followed by the economy at 20%, immigration at 9%, and Afghanistan at 5% [180]

179.   https://www.dailywire.com/news/i-will-not-comply-social-media-erupts-over-biden-vaccine-mandate-speech
180.   https://www.breitbart.com/politics/2021/09/10/cnn-two-percent-think-america-doing-very-well-joe-biden/

SEPTEMBER 10 – DOCTOR JOE KNOWS BEST

Biden tells students at a Washington, D.C. middle school that he will invite them to the White House if they all get vaccinated.

"For students here at Brookland, once you all get vaccinated, you're invited to a special visit at the White House. Maybe let you fly the helicopters. I'm only joking about that."

Biden encourages parents to vaccinate children 12 and over, despite the fact children statistically do not face severe effects from COVID, and there is a demonstrated elevated risk of heart inflammation, particularly to teen boys and young men.

"The safest thing you can do for your child 12 and over is get them vaccinated," he said. "That's it. Simple, plain, straightforward. ... You've got them vaccinated for all kinds of other things — measles, mumps, rubella."

The Federal Government under Joe Biden is stepping out of its Constitutional bounds once again and attempting to control our lives. Here we have the President of the United States, with no medical training whatsoever, giving parents and children potentially dangerous medical advice unchecked. [181]

---

181.   https://www.breitbart.com/   politics/2021/09/10/joe-biden-invites-children-to-the-white-house-if-their-school-gets-vaccinated/

SEPTEMBER 10 – UNLAWFUL SEARCH AND SEIZURE

Unconstitutional behavior abounds as Biden invents a way to monitor Americans' bank accounts and financial transactions to target tax evasion. Even more egregious is that banks are told they do not even have to disclose to their customers the reporting of their financial transactions to the government!

Biden receives wide criticism for wildly violating the 4th Amendment, which prohibits unlawful search and seizure.

Patrick Hedger, vice President of policy at the Taxpayers' Protection Alliance, criticized the plan, saying, "The IRS is first and foremost, a law enforcement agency and the Fourth Amendment protects against unreasonable searches and seizures in pursuit of, of looking for wrongdoing and criminal actions, so I think this is going to run into severe Fourth Amendment headwinds."[182]

"The proposal would require banks to report to gross inflows and outflows to the IRS, including transactions from Venmo, PayPal, crypto exchanges and the like in an effort to fight tax evasion," the Daily Mail reported, adding, "The IRS would know how much money is in an individual's bank account in a given year, whether the individual earned

---

182.   https://www.dailywire.com/news/biden-dems-want-to-moni-tor-americans-bank-accounts-blasted-as-violating-4th-amendment

income on that account and exactly how much was going in and out." [183]

SEPTEMBER 11 – THE 20ᵀᴴ ANNIVERSARY OF 9/11

Biden goes to New York City to visit Ground Zero and commemorate the 20th anniversary of the September 11 attacks. He was a Senator when the four jets were highjacked by terrorists twenty years ago, prompting our nation's longest war.

After his visit at Ground Zero, Biden went to the sacred field near Shanksville, Pennsylvania, where Todd Beamer and other heroic passengers prevented the weaponized jet from reaching D.C. Finally, Biden visited the Pentagon, where terrorists struck the heart of our mighty military.

America and the world have never been the same since that fateful day. President George W. Bush, who was in office during the attacks, said, "So much of our politics has become a naked appeal to anger, fear and resentment. On America's day of trial and grief, I saw millions of people instinctively grab their neighbor's hand and rally to the cause of one another. That is the America know. It is the truest version of ourselves. It is what we have been and what we can be again." [184]

---

183.   https://www.dailymail.co.uk/news/article-9973671/Bidens-plan-let-IRS-SNOOP-bank-accounts.html
184.   https://www.cbsnews.com/news/biden-obama-clinton-911-new-york-display-of-unity/

SEPTEMBER 14 – KING BIDEN III?

More than a dozen State Governors put out a statement condemning Biden's unconstitutional vaccine mandate. Arizona, however, is the first state to sue the Biden Administration.

Arizona Attorney General Mark Brnovich said, "The federal government cannot force people to get the COVID-19 vaccine. The Biden Administration is once again flouting our laws and precedents to push their radical agenda. There can be no serious or scientific discussion about containing the spread of COVID-19 that doesn't begin at our southern border."

"Under our Constitution, the President is not a king who can exercise this sort of unbridled power unilaterally. And even George III wouldn't have dreamed that he could enact such sweeping policies by royal decree alone," Brnovich argued.

According to a press release from the Arizona attorney general's office, Brnovich's lawsuit makes the case that "Biden's vaccine mandate violates the Equal Protection Clause by favoring migrants that have crossed into the country illegally over legal U.S. citizens. The Biden Administration allows migrants to decline the vaccine, protecting their freedom and bodily autonomy more than American citizens."

Lawsuits may be the least of Biden's challenges, as even the Occupational Safety and Health Administration (OSHA) is not remotely equipped to enforce Biden's unconstitutional mandate. [185]

SEPTEMBER 17 – CBP IS OVERWHELMED WITH MIGRANTS

Both international bridges in Del Rio, Texas, are closed due to the migrant crisis. A sudden influx of migrants necessitated the closure as over 12,000 mostly Haitian illegal immigrants were held under one of the bridges. This has overwhelmed the city, as the migrant population is nearly half that of the city itself.

Customs and Border Patrol issue a written statement today: "U.S. Customs and Border Protection today announced that the Office of Field Operations (OFO) Del Rio Port of Entry will temporarily close and re-route traffic from Del Rio to Eagle Pass to more effectively manage resources and ensure uninterrupted flow of trade and travel. Consistent with established cross border travel management procedures, traffic that normally uses the Amistad Dam International Bridge and the Del Rio International Bridge will be directed 57 miles east to the Eagle Pass Port of Entry."

"This temporary closure and shift is necessary in order for CBP to respond to urgent safety and security needs presented by an influx of migrants into Del Rio and is

---

185.   https://www.dailywire.com/news/arizona-files-first-lawsuit-over-biden-vaccine-mandate

effective immediately," the statement continued. "It will advance and protect national interests and help ensure the safety of the traveling public, commercial traffic, and CBP employees and facilities." [186]

Del Rio Mayor Bruno Lozano declared a state of disaster and shut down the toll booths on the Del Rio International Bridge and closed it to traffic stating, "Dire circumstances require dire responses," according to the Texas Tribune. "There's people having babies down there [under the bridge], there's people collapsing out of the heat. They're pretty aggressive, rightly so — they've been in the heat day after day after day." [187]

SEPTEMBER 17 – WHAT WOULD REAGAN DO?

Biden leaves for his vacation house in Rehoboth Beach—a visit that was repeatedly delayed in August. This will be the first time he has visited the property, for which he paid $2.74 million in 2017, since the First Lady's birthday in June. He faced criticism for going on vacation while Americans remain trapped in Afghanistan, fearing for their lives at the hands of a vengeful Taliban bent on destroying anyone who had any connection to America over the past 20 years.

186.   https://www.breitbart.com/border/2021/09/17/cbp-closes-both-international-bridges-in-del-rio-texas-as-migrant-camp-crisis-worsens/

187.   https://www.breitbart.com/border/2021/09/17/tex-as-border-mayor-declares-disaster-closes-entry-to-internation-al-bridge-above-migrant-camp/

The State Department has confirmed that Americans are still stuck in Afghanistan and blames the Taliban for blocking the flights. "To our minds, these flights, these individuals, there is no reason they should not be able to depart," State Department spokesman Ned Price told reporters. "And that's what we're continuing to focus on."

The obvious question is why weren't civilian evacuations completed prior to the military withdrawal?

If Ronald Reagan were alive and in office today, something tells me he would have done everything in his power to rescue these Americans. [188]

SEPTEMBER 19 – A MASSIVE BLOW TO BIDEN

Senate Parliamentarian Elizabeth Macdonough bars Biden admin and Democrats from adding pathway to citizenship for illegal immigrants to $3.5 trillion spending bill.

To add salt to Biden's wound, Senator Joe Manchin (D-WV) wants to delay the vote until 2022. Axios reported that "Manchin's new timeline — if he insists on it — would disrupt the plans by House Speaker Nancy Pelosi (D-Calif.) and Senate Majority Leader Chuck Schumer (D-N.Y.) to vote on the budget reconciliation package this month."

---

188.   https://www.breitbart.com/politics/2021/09/17/joe-biden-leaving-for-beach-vacation-even-as-americans-remain-stuck-in-afghanistan/

On a personal note, my conservative family has generally supported Joe Manchin over the years. My father recalls the time that Joe Manchin, of Manchin Carpets, laid carpet in our home in West Virginia decades ago. My Republican father and his Republican business partner have met with Joe Manchin and have even had taken a photo together.

Manchin is one of the most powerful Senators in D.C. because of his moderate stance on several issues, which reflects the complex political views of many West Virginians. My immediate family has always been Republican, which was a minority position in the State of West Virginia in the past.

However, the old-school Democrats were basically God-fearing, gun-toting, and pro-Union. Political debate boiled down to labor vs. management because of the coal mining industry. WV Democrats were and are still nothing like the radical Left today, which is embodied by the likes of Bernie Sanders and Alexandria Ocasia-Cortez. [189]

SEPTEMBER 21 – BIDEN BUSTED FOR REFUSING TO ANSWER REPORTERS

The White House Press Pool files formal complaint against Biden for refusing to answer media questions regarding the many crises his Administration has presided over.

---

189.   https://www.dailywire.com/news/big-blow-to-biden-senate-parliamentarian-rules-citizenship-path-for-illegals-cannot-be-in-3-5-trillion-bill-report-says

It all started after Biden met with British Prime Minister Boris Johnson. The British are also infuriated over Biden's failed withdrawal from Afghanistan.

Senior White House & Political Correspondent Ed O' Keeffe tweeted, "IN THE OVAL OFFICE... @POTUS Biden and British PM @BorisJohnson meet to discuss pandemic, trade and other issues. Johnson took 3 questions. White House aides shouted down U.S. attempts to ask questions. I asked Biden about southern border and we couldn't decipher what he said." [190]

Association President Steven Portnoy said in a statement, "The entire editorial component of the U.S. pool went immediately into Jen Psaki's office to register a formal complaint that no American reporters were recognized for questions in the President's Oval Office, and that wranglers loudly shouted over the President as he seemed to give an answer to Ed O'Keefe's question about the situation at the Southern Border," the statement said. "Biden's answer could not be heard over the shouting." [191]

This comes as no surprise since it's been reported that Biden ran his Presidential campaign from his basement! Biden's handlers ensure that he always stays on script, and anyone or anything that threatens to expose his cognitive deficiencies is stopped by his gatekeepers.

---

190.   https://twitter.com/edokeefe
191.   https://www.dailywire.com/news/white-house-reporters-file-

SEPTEMBER 27 – A FAKE WHITE HOUSE?

As if Biden's election wasn't bizarre enough, he's now been caught staging photo ops in a fake White House!

That's right. Biden is filmed receiving his vaccine booster shot in a set that was made to look like it was coming from the White House... the set is actually in the South Court Auditorium in the Eisenhower Executive Office Building across the street from the actual White House!

This came after a D.C. citizen claims to have looked into an empty Rose Garden where a supposedly live airing was taking place.[192]

These odd "created sets instead of the real thing" raise questions about the Biden Administration's media strategy, and why it was easier to broadcast from a set rather than the real White House where Biden [allegedly] lives and works. [193]

Here's something to ponder... If the White House staff believes it better to film Biden from the fake set, is Biden really occupying the White House and running our country or is someone else? Think about it.

formal-complaint-against-biden-for-refusing-to-answer-questions
192.   https://www.youtube.com/watch?v=DIP9dYtyJvc
193.   https://www.breitbart.com/politics/2021/09/30/fake-views-white-house-creates-illusionary-white-house-set-for-joe-biden-events/

SEPTEMBER 27 – VACCINE OBSESSION

Biden says that we can get back to normal when 98% of Americans are vaccinated. "Look, I think we get the vast majority — like is going on in so many – some industries and some schools — 96, 97, 98 percent," Biden claimed. "One thing for certain: A quarter of the country can't go unvaccinated and us not continue to have a problem," he said.

Biden believes that the coronavirus pandemic is "a pandemic of the unvaccinated." He went on to beg, "Please, please do the right thing. Please get the shots. And it can save your life." If it is so life-saving why aren't more people breaking down the doors to obtain the shots?

And if it is perfectly safe for everyone, why are the Big Pharma companies liability-free for any potential issues that could arise as a result of being vaccinated? If something is safe, why does it need to be exempt from liability? So many have pointed out that this could be a concern to some who have not yet decided to pursue vaccination.

Back in August, Fauci said, "If we keep lingering without getting those people vaccinated that should be vaccinated, this thing could linger on, leading to the development of another variant which could complicate things." In February, Fauci said that as long as 70-85% of the population were vaccinated, the country could get back to normal.

Given that 77% of Americans had at least one shot at this point, despite easy availability, it shows Biden's number is clearly in the realm of fantasy. It is also far above that given by any health authority. Norway, for example, relaxed restrictions once 76% of the population was vaccinated. [194] Why is America demanding 98%?

SEPTEMBER 28 — LIAR-IN-CHIEF

Biden faces backlash after Generals' testimony directly contradict Biden's own claims about the Afghanistan withdrawal fiasco last month. Contrary to what he said, Biden *had* received recommendations to keep several thousand American troops in Afghanistan, advice he denied receiving.

Testifying under oath, US Central Command Gen. Kenneth McKenzie said that the US needed to "maintain 2,500 troops in Afghanistan" and that withdrawing those forces would "lead inevitably to the collapse of the Afghan military forces and eventually the Afghan government."

Here's a telling excerpt from an interview with George Stephanopoulos on August 19th:

> STEPHANOPOULOS: "No one told — your military advisors did not tell you, 'No, we should just keep 2,500 troops. It's been a stable situation for the last

---

194.   https://www.breitbart.com/politics/2021/09/27/joe-biden-we-need-up-to-98-vaccination-rate-before-we-go-back-to-normal/

several years. We can do that. We can continue to do that'?

BIDEN: No. No one said that to me that I can recall. Look, George, the reason why it's been stable for a year is because the last President said, 'We're leaving. And here's the deal I wanna make with you, Taliban. We're agreeing to leave if you agree not to attack us between now and the time we leave on May the 1st.' [195]

Either Biden is lying, or he is not fit to hold the highest Office in the land. It's becoming clear it is just that simple.

SEPTEMBER 29 – OBAMA CRITICIZES BIDEN

Biden receives criticism from Former President Barack Obama over his immigration policy. He said that having "open borders" is "unsustainable."

During an interview with Good Morning America co-anchor Robin Roberts, Obama said that the ghastly images of 15,000 illegal aliens being trapped under a bridge in Del Rio, Texas was "a painful reminder that we don't have this right yet and we've got more work to do."

Obama called Biden "big-hearted," but said that it was time to "get serious about dealing with this problem in a systemic

---

195.   https://www.dailywire.com/news/biden-lied-President-blasted-after-top-generals-directly-contradict-what-biden-said-about-afghanistan

way, as opposed to these one-offs where we're constantly reacting to emergencies."

"Immigration is tough. It always has been because, on the one hand, I think we are naturally a people that wants to help others. And we see tragedy and hardship and families that are desperately trying to get here so that their kids are safe, and they're in some cases fleeing violence or catastrophe. At the same time, we're a nation state. We have borders. The idea that we can just have open borders is something that ... as a practical matter, is unsustainable." [196]

Ouch. You know it's bad when Obama distances himself from his former Veep!

SEPTEMBER 29 – ARE MASKS ONLY FOR SHOW?

Even though Biden has had three Pfizer shots, he virtue-signals by wearing his mask indoors and outdoors. Today, however, he is caught mask-less at the annual Congressional baseball game.

He even embraced Nancy Pelosi, who was also mask-less. Despite public messaging pushing masks and social distancing, and the continued mandates for government employees and all who utilize public transportation, Biden is far from the only proponent who is inconsistent at best when practicing his own recommendations. [197]

196.   https://www.dailywire.com/news/obama-takes-shot-at-bi-den-the-idea-that-we-can-just-have-open-borders-is-unsustainable
197.   https://www.breitbart.com/politics/2021/09/30/mask-erade-

I trust history will record this charade for what it really is.
Make sure you are on the right side of history.

CHAPTER 10

OCTOBER 2021: THE "LET'S GO, BRANDON!" CHANT IS BORN

OCTOBER 2 – BRANDON BECOMES THE MOST POPULAR NAME ON EARTH

NASCAR driver Brandon Brown wins his first Xfinity Series race at Talladega today. Like many other sporting events across the country, the chant "F--k Joe Biden!" broke out among fans in the stands.

It happened again while Brandon Brown was being interviewed on live TV after the race was over. As a form of damage control, NBC Sports Reporter Kelli Stavast claimed that the crowd was actually chanting "Let's Go, Brandon!"

Perhaps she really didn't hear it correctly, but it's fairly obvious what is being said when you watch the interview on YouTube! [198]

Either way, America didn't buy it. There's only so much the mainstream media can do to prop up and protect Joe Biden.

As a result, "Let's Go, Brandon!" has become a euphemism for "F--k Joe Biden," a social media meme, a plethora of Conservative merch, and even the title of this book!

---

198.   https://youtu.be/axcmVFtwSM4

OCTOBER 2 – BIDEN RETREATS TO DELAWARE

On the same day that the viral "Let's Go, Brandon!" chant is born, Biden retreats to his vacation home in Wilmington, Delaware...again!

Frustrations over his failure to bring Democrats together to pass his sweeping $3.5 trillion government-overhaul bill have caught up to him. Republicans are staunchly opposed to and Democrats cannot agree on the particulars. [199]

OCTOBER 5 – BIDEN RECEIVES A CHILLY RECEPTION IN MICHIGAN

On the road to push his massive $3.5 trillion dollar plan, Biden arrives in Howell, Michigan, where he is greeted by protestors holding "F--k Joe Biden" signs. Irritated by the signs Biden claims he has a mandate to implement his "Build Back Better" agenda. "Not withstanding some of the signs I saw coming in ... that's why 81 million Americans voted for me," Biden said. "The largest number of votes in American history — a clear majority!" [200]

Funny how it seems the majority of the country is actually chanting for you to go, Joe.

199. https://www.troyrecord.com/2021/10/02/everybody-is-frus-trated-biden-says-as-his-agenda-stalls/
200. https://www.dailywire.com/news/irritated-biden-addresses-f-joe-biden-signs-after-chilly-reception-in-michigan

OCTOBER 6 — FAKE WHITE HOUSE SET EXPLAINED

All of us are asking the same question: Why does Biden use bizarre fake sets instead of a real room in the White House for his broadcasts?

Abigail Marone, press secretary for Missouri Republican Sen. Josh Hawley asks, "Why did the White House build a literal game show set complete with fake windows for Joe Biden??? So weird," on Twitter.

Conservative commentator and podcast host Benny Johnson also asked Twitter, "Why does Joe Biden feel the need to use a Fake White House set across the street from the actual White House."

A "Truman Show Presidency," tweeted Human Events Senior Editor Jack Posobiec.

Stephen Miller, a former Trump advisor, offers a theory. Miller said on Twitter, "The reason Biden uses this bizarre virtual set for televised meetings — and not an actual room like East Room, Cabinet, Oval, Roosevelt, Sit Room, etc. — is because it allows him to read a script directly from a face-on monitor (& w/out teleprompter glass that can be seen on camera)." [201]

---

201.   https://www.dailywire.com/news/trump-adviser-offers-theo-ry-on-why-biden-uses-fake-white-house-set

So in order to read a script, the President of the United States of America and one of the world's most powerful leaders has to present from a stage. Got it.

OCTOBER 6 – BIDEN'S APPROVAL RATING PLUMMETS TO AN ALL-TIME LOW

According to a Quinnipiac University poll, Biden's approval rating falls to 38%, the lowest since he took office. Polling analyst Tim Malloy pointed out the obvious, "Battered on trust, doubted on leadership, and challenged on overall competency, President Biden is being hammered on all sides as his approval rating continues its downward slide to a number not seen since the tough scrutiny of the Trump Administration."

According to the poll:

- the response to the coronavirus: 48 percent approve, while 50 percent disapprove;

- the economy: 39 percent approve, while 55 percent disapprove;

- his job as Commander in Chief of the U.S. military: 37 percent approve, while 58 percent disapprove;

- taxes: 37 percent approve, while 54 percent disapprove;

- foreign policy: 34 percent approve, while 58 percent disapprove;

- immigration issues: 25 percent approve, while 67 percent disapprove;

- the situation at the Mexican border: 23 percent approve, while 67 percent disapprove [202]

OCTOBER 8 – BIDEN ATTACKS AN ITALIAN-AMERICAN HOLIDAY

In his Columbus Day statement, Biden highlights the "painful history of wrongs and atrocities that many European explorers inflicted on Tribal Nations and Indigenous communities." [203]

I am going to honor my Uncle Gene Vallorani, by quoting his perspective as an Italian-American on Columbus Day:

> "Liberals everywhere seek to destroy Columbus and replace his "day" with "Indigenous Peoples Day." There is nothing wrong with a day to celebrate native Americans. The real issue is the liberal's insistence on taking away a day that Italian-Americans view as a celebration of the achievements made to build this great country of ours. Thus the below: Italian American

> For decades Italian-Americans have taken pride in celebrating Columbus Day in the United States, and rightfully so. Not because of some modern claims

202.   https://www.dailywire.com/news/hammered-on-all-sides-bidens-approval-plummets-to-lowest-level-of-presidency
203.   https://www.whitehouse.gov/briefing-room/Presidential-actions/2021/10/08/a-proclamation-on-columbus-day-2021/

of white Europeans committing genocide against Native Americans, but because the Italian American experience in the United States is one of the most unique events in American History.

It has been said no group of immigrants to the United States has so quickly and wholeheartedly embraced and transitioned into becoming Americans. The Italian love affair with America began long before the great migration of the late 19th and early 20th centuries. This is because, before the 1860s, there was no Italian nation per se.

The Italian peninsula was a series of kingdoms dominated by France, Spain, or the Papal States. With no national identity until the late 19th Century, Italians yearned to be free, and part of a country committed to freedom and justice for all. This is why they came to America in such large numbers. Yet, the Italian story in America actually began long before with the early adventurers who, like Columbus, did participate in North America's European explorations.

Americans of Italian descent fought in the American Revolution, as Texans with Sam Houston at the battle of San Jacinto against Santa Anna, helping win Texas Independence from Mexico, the Civil War, and every other war for freedom and liberty waged by the then young United States.

While modern Hollywood consistently portrays Italian-Americans as members of the Mafia, Cosa

Nostra, and any other vile persona, the truth is most Italian-Americans have always clung to a strong faith in God and the importance of preserving strong family ties.

The celebration of Columbus Day is recognizing these values and a time of celebration in honoring those ancestors who arrived before them and who have ingrained generations of family values for many, many Americans of Italian ancestry.

To deny Italian Americans pride in their heritage by destroying the celebration of Columbus Day due to the misconception of Native American genocide is a false narrative and extremely unjust. Christopher Columbus was a religious individual who actually defended the native populations of the New World. According to historians, Columbus was struck by the beauty and gentleness of the people he found upon his arrival in the Americas. The first Native Americans, according to diaries of the time, were so trusting and kind, Columbus made efforts to prevent any of his crew members from taking advantage of the natives.

The stories are too long to tell all of them in this brief missive but, let it suffice to say, of all the early explorers, many were Italian, and none ravaged the Native Americans. The same cannot be said for other European explorers, but to single out Christopher Columbus and deprive those of us descended from our ancestors who helped make America great not having a day set aside to celebrate and take pride in that part of our ancestry is unnecessary and unfair.

Happy Columbus Day, everyone, and God Bless America, the last great hope of mankind." [204]

OCTOBER 9 – ITALIANS CHANT "F--K JOE BIDEN!"

Thousands of protestors in Rome chant "F—k Joe Biden!" rather than the less offensive "Let's Go, Brandon!" chant as they march down Via Veneto past the U.S. Embassy.

According to the Associated Press, the demonstrators were "clashing with police" as they protested Italy's new 'Green Pass' vaccination requirement for employees to enter their offices. The certification is mandatory beginning Oct. 15 and applies to both public and private workplaces.

Both employees and employers risk fines if they don't comply. Public sector workers can be suspended if they show up to work five times without a Green Pass.

The pass is already required in Italy to enter museums, theaters, gyms, and even to eat in indoor restaurants, as well as to take long-distance trains and buses or domestic flights," the wire service reported. [205]

---

204.   https://lidblog.com/columbus-day-italian-americans/
205.   https://www.dailywire.com/news/going-global-protesters-in-rome-chant-f-joe-biden

OCTOBER 12 – SOUTHWEST AIRLINES HIT HARD BY VACCINE MANDATE

Southwest Airlines CEO, Gary Kelly, blames Biden's mandate for their vaccination mandate, which goes against Texas governor Greg Abbott's ban on mandates in Texas. Even though Southwest is based in Dallas, Texas, they are also a federal contractor and directly targeted by the mandates.

CEO Gary Kelly went on record to say that he personally opposes vaccinate mandates in an interview with CNBC. "I've never been in favor of corporations imposing that kind of a mandate. I'm not in favor of that, never have been. But the executive order from President Biden mandates that all federal employees and then all federal contractors, which covers all major airlines, have to have a vaccine mandate in place by December 8. So we're working through that."

It was a rough weekend for Southwest as they had to cancel more than 1,800 flights. 350 more were cancelled on Monday. The company denied that this had anything to do with vaccine mandates and blamed the weather and traffic control challenges instead. But other major airlines had no such issues.

This shows that the leadership from Washington, whether good or bad, has real effects on businesses and citizens. [206]

---

206. https://www.dailywire.com/news/southwest-ceo-blames-joe-biden-for-airlines-vaccine-mandate

OCTOBER 16 – BARE SHELVES BIDEN

Biden faces intense criticism over the supply chain crisis, as container ships are stranded in California harbors and 97% of retailers are affected by shortages.

Biden is called 'Bare Shelves Biden' and criticized over his lack of action. Former Walmart CEO Bill Simon said, "I've never seen it like this, and I don't really think anybody living in this country has. I mean, this is really unprecedented" during an interview on Fox Business.

Simon explained during an interview on "Mornings with Maria" that "there's a shortage of labor in our distribution system and there's a shortage of people to put [items] on the shelf." He believes the crisis will not be relieved "until we alleviate the labor shortage that's out there and get people driving trucks and unloading at the docks and stocking shelves." [207]

At one point in October, Biden raised eyebrows when he stated the supply chain fiasco could be resolved if truckers would drive at night. How out of touch *is* he? [208]

Industry leaders have been begging President Biden and Transportation Secretary Pete Buttigieg to facilitate

207.   https://www.dailywire.com/news/unprecedented-former-walmart-ceo-blasts-biden-for-supply-chain-crisis
208.   https://flagandcross.com/biden-raises-eyebrows-with-wild-plan-to-fix-supply-chain-truckers-can-drive-at-night/

American supply chains return to normalcy for the past several months.

Matthew Shay, President and CEO of the National Retail Federation, wrote a letter to Biden where he pleads:

> "The congestion issues have not only added days and weeks to our supply chains but have led to inventory shortages impacting our ability to serve our customers.

> "In addition, these delays have added significant transportation and warehousing costs for retailers."

> "Our nation's supply chains are stressed because of the COVID-19 global pandemic, and they continue to struggle through our economic recovery.

> "We would like an opportunity to discuss the impact these issues are having on the nation's retailers, our workers and our customers, as well as potential solutions to address current and future disruptions.

> "We need strong leadership from the Administration to galvanize attention to the current situation as well as work to resolve long-standing issues that limit safe and efficient port operations." [209]

Unfortunately, Politico reported that Transportation Secretary Buttigieg has been on paid paternity leave for months as he and his "husband" adopted twins.

---

209.   https://chainstoreage.com/nrf-biden-please-fix-supply-chain

"While U.S. ports faced anchor-to-anchor traffic and Congress nearly melted down over the President's infrastructure bill in recent weeks, the usually omnipresent Transportation secretary was lying low. They didn't previously announce it, but Buttigieg's office told West Wing Playbook that the secretary has actually been on paid leave since mid-August to spend time with his husband, Chasten, and their two newborn babies." [210]

This is what the beginning the end looks like, folks. Elections have consequences, "rigged" or otherwise.

The country is in crisis and the person responsible for one major aspect of our daily lives being handled is out – and apparently indefinitely – on tax-payer-paid leave.

OCTOBER 16 – THE BIDENS CAUGHT BREAKING D.C. RULES

D.C. rules state masks must be worn inside restaurants, when not eating or drinking: "Everyone (including fully vaccinated people) must wear masks [in]... restaurants and bars (when not eating or drinking)."

Yet Joe Biden and his wife Jill were photographed in a Michelin-starred fine dining Italian restaurant, Fiola Mare, for their date night. The Secret Service members escorting them were, of course, wearing masks.

210.   https://www.politico.com/newsletters/west-wing-play-book/2021/10/14/can-pete-buttigieg-have-it-all-494710

The rules that Democrats impose on the rest of us are so cumbersome that even they cannot follow them. But the Democrats seem to see themselves as above everyone else, and therefore above the rules they set in place for the rest of us. [211]

OCTOBER 21 – TEXAS AND MISSOURI SUE BIDEN ADMINISTRATION

Texas Attorney General Ken Paxton announces the intentions of the State of Texas to sue the Biden Administration over money earmarked to build the border wall in order to force its appropriate expenditure.

The Texas Tribune reported, "On Inauguration Day, Biden ordered a pause on all border wall construction and an assessment of federal government contracts already awarded for the project, calling former President Donald Trump's signature promise a 'waste of money' and saying that it was 'not a serious policy solution.' The lawsuit, filed against Biden and Department of Homeland Security Secretary Alejandro Mayorkas in the U.S. district court in Victoria, argues that Congress had set aside $1.375 billion to construct barriers along the southwest border and that the Biden Administration doesn't have the constitutional authority to refuse to spend money that Congress authorized for border wall construction."[212]

211.   https://www.newsweek.com/joe-jill-biden-maskless-dc-restaurant-video-photos-1639760

212.   https://www.texastribune.org/2021/10/21/texas-paxton-bor-

Standing near the Texas and Mexico border, Paxton said,

> "Well, thank you all for coming. As you can see,
> we're in El Paso, a great city in Texas with the border
> wall behind us and the attorney general of Missouri,
> Eric Schmidt, he's a good friend of mine, he's come
> down to announce with us — and I'm going to let
> him say his own words — that we will be filing a
> lawsuit against the Biden Administration as it relates
> to building this wall."

> "The fact that Congress appropriated large sums of
> money and directed that that money be spent on the
> wall, our lawsuit is about forcing that expenditure to
> be spent the way Congress intended. And the reason
> we care so much about this is [that] it is having tre-
> mendously negative effects on our states, I'll let Eric
> tell you what he's doing in Missouri, but obviously
> tremendous social costs, much higher crime, we've
> got the cartels on our border who are human traf-
> ficking and [filing] people through here. As you
> know, these people don't get here for free."

> "They have to pay the cartels and as a result, Border
> Patrol and many of our law enforcement are busy
> dealing with a lot of people, record numbers of
> people. I think the numbers are up over 300% from
> just a year ago under the Trump Administration
> and that is forcing Border Patrol to spend a lot more
> time on more logistics as opposed to stopping the
> importation of drugs like Fentanyl, which is killing
> people and will kill people all over the country and

der-wall-lawsuit-biden/

so it's having tremendous social cost, but it also has tremendous economic costs for my state and for Missouri." [213]

Kudos to Ken Paxton and Eric Schmidt for holding the Biden Administration accountable. As the author and artist Doug Giles, who is my friend and co-author on the book *Would Jesus Vote for Trump?* would say, "Go, Tehas!"

OCTOBER 21 – BIDEN VS. THE NAVY SEALS

The Biden Administration threatens to force unvaccinated Navy SEALs with a reduction in salary, forcing them to pay for their own training and removing them from special warfare!

The directive states, "The Vice Chief of Naval Operations retains authority for non-judicial punishment and courts-martial. Involuntary extension of enlistments is not authorized on the basis of administrative or disciplinary action for vaccination refusal. The CCDA may seek recoupment of applicable bonuses, special and incentive pays, and the cost of training and education for service members refusing the vaccine."

Review what this unclassified Navy document entails:

---

213.   https://www.dailywire.com/news/lets-go-brandon-well-see-you-in-court-texas-ag-paxton-slams-biden-files-suit-against-biden-administration-over-border-wall

2. Policy. In order to maximize readiness, it is the policy goal of the U.S. Navy to achieve a fully vaccinated force against the persistent and lethal threat of COVID-19.

2.a. In support of the above stated policy, and as directed by the Secretary of the Navy's lawful order, the Navy has commenced a mandatory vaccination campaign per references (a) through (c). Navy service members refusing the COVID-19 vaccination, absent a pending or approved exemption, shall be processed for administrative separation per this NAVADMIN and supporting references. To ensure a fair and consistent process, separation determinations will be centralized under the CCDA as outlined in the paragraphs below. [214]

Threatening our military's strength by penalizing some of our best elite service members in our Armed Forces drew heavy criticism from former and current military members.

Interior Secretary Ryan Zinke, a former Navy SEAL, blasted Biden on Facebook:

"Our Nation's best don't sign up to be a Navy SEAL to cash in on our training years later. We give a blood oath to fight for freedom and defend the Constitution against all enemies, both foreign and domestic. In doing so, we bear a burden of emotional, psychological, physical, and family stress of constant

---

214. https://www.mynavyhr.navy.mil/Portals/55/Messages/NA-VADMIN/NAV2021/NAV21225.txt

deployments and low pay because we love our Country. Shame Mr. President for not recognizing the service and sacrifice and further insulting SEALs by making this about money."

Michael Berry, First Liberty Institute's general counsel and Lt. Col. U.S. Marine Corps Reserve, who represents approximately 34 active-duty SEALs and two reservists told Fox News:

> "Purging our military of its elite servicemembers is detrimental to national security. Doing so because the Commander in Chief refuses to accommodate their religious convictions is abhorrent to the Constitution. Their years of experience and leadership in service to our nation is immeasurable and irreplaceable. ... Remove a SEAL from special warfare, reduce his salary, and force him to repay his training is purely vindictive and punitive. And it's illegal. They have nothing to do with a virus." [215]

OCTOBER 21 – ANDERSON COOPER TO THE RESCUE

CNN's Anderson Cooper had to give substantial help to get Biden through his CNN town hall, which was filled with bizarre and concerning moments, and seemed to show the President in significant mental decline. At one point Biden asked, "What am I doing here?"

---

215.   https://www.dailywire.com/news/bidens-defense-dept-could-make-unvaxxed-navy-seals-pay-for-their-training-trumps-interior-sec-a-former-navy-seal-blasts-biden

We are all wondering the same thing, Joe.

Anderson jumped in and helped him remember the name of the port city. As Anderson spoke, Biden was seen standing awkwardly still and holding out his clenched fists as if he wanted to pound something. At another point, he stood stiffly allowing his arms to hang with his head bowed down. Several times Biden had to stop and close his eyes as he tried to finish a statement.

Biden also made the "OK" symbol with his hand and peered through it, whispering like he did in a press conference earlier this year. To be honest, it was painful to watch even as a Republican. I am embarrassed for Joe Biden, his family, and those who voted for him. I am unsure how much longer he will be fit for office. [216]

It makes you wonder if this farce is considered to be elderly abuse.

OCTOBER 22 – 1.6 MILLION PEOPLE ARRESTED AT THE BORDER

US Customs and Border Protection (CBP) released figures that showed 1.6 million people were arrested at the border, the highest number ever recorded.

---

216.   https://www.breitbart.com/politics/2021/10/22/someone-re-boot-biden-8-awkward-moments-as-joe-biden-struggled-through-cnn-town-hall/

Laura Collins, an immigration expert at the George W. Bush Institute, said "I don't think it's going to slow down anytime soon." People are escaping desperate economic situations in Latin America because of COVID-19, authoritarian regimes, gang violence, weather, etc.

Plus there's 82 million refugees displaced from their homes worldwide, 15,000 Haitian migrants in Del Rio, and an intense number of unaccompanied minors at the Southern border. It's a convergence of several factors that are overwhelming CBP. [217]

OCTOBER 23 – BIDEN ADMINISTRATION DENIES KNOWLEDGE OF "LET'S GO, BRANDON!"

Biden Administration claims ignorance about the popular "Let's Go, Brandon!" slogan, indicating they're either lying or have not watched any sporting events, been on Twitter, or watched the news all month.

According to the Washington Post, "Administration officials sought to downplay the phenomenon, and at least one claimed to be unfamiliar with the 'Let's Go, Brandon!' chant or its cruder cousin, though they are now chanted everywhere from football stadiums to concert arenas to local bars."

---

217. https://www.wsj.com/articles/border-patrol-makes-about-1-66-million-arrests-at-southern-border-in-2021-fiscal-year-11634932866

I certainly can't blame the Administration for handling it this way. Aside from fixing the colossal mess they've made in this country, ignoring it and hoping it goes away is probably their best strategy. [218]

OCTOBER 25 – FORMER OBAMA ADVISOR CRITICIZES BIDEN

Former Obama economic advisor Larry Summers sounds the alarm over Biden's runaway inflation. "Now we see inflation becoming more widespread in a wider range of products, spreading to the housing and labor markets. I have been alarmed for a long time, and I'm more alarmed now. ... We're in more danger than we have been during my career of losing control of inflation in the U.S."

Treasury Secretary Janet Yellen, responded to Summers' concerns on CNN's State of the Union, "We are going through a period of inflation that's higher than Americans have seen in a long time. And it's something that's obviously a concern and worrying them. But we haven't lost control."

Summers responded to Yellen on Twitter, saying, "She expresses confidence that inflation is decelerating and will be back to target levels by the end of next year. I hope she is right, but I think it's much less than a 50/50 chance."

---

218.   https://www.washingtonpost.com/politics/biden-vul-gar-signs-chants/2021/10/22/6071836e-3122-11ec-a880-a9d-8c009a0b1_story.html

"I began my career when Paul Volker was taking over at the Fed and not since then have I been more worried. I am curious at what point in the last 40 years Treasury thinks the risk of an inflation spiral are greater than they are now. When the Administration formulated its budget in February, it expected 2 percent inflation in 2021, I was warning about inflation. Their forecast is no longer operative. In May and June, @SecYellen expressed confidence that inflation would be back to the 2 percent range by late 2021 or early 2022. Now, this forecast is no longer operative."

This is yet another example that Biden's critics are not always conservative. [219]

OCTOBER 25 – FIRST "LET'S GO, BRANDON!" MASK WORN ON HOUSE FLOOR

Olivia Beavers of Politico, tweeted, "Spotted at House votes: GOP Rep. Jeff Duncan of SC wearing a mask with a phrase that Republicans are using in place of F--k Joe Biden." [220]

Humorless Democrats criticized him. Back in South Carolina, Oconee Democratic Party chairwoman Jody Gaulin was furious.

219.   https://www.dailywire.com/news/top-obama-eco-nomic-adviser-torches-biden-admin-over-skyrocketing-infla-tion-my-alarm-is-increasing
220.   https://twitter.com/Olivia_Beavers/sta-tus/1452793951715475466

The chairwoman told The Seneca Journal, "Not only does Jeff Duncan not deliver for the people of the third district—I cannot think of a thing he has truly done—he now sports a vulgar slogan on his mask and walks off the floor! The hypocrisy of the Faith and Freedom BBQ is exposed!" the Democrat raged. [221]

OCTOBER 25 – BIDEN HAS NOW TAKEN MORE VACATIONS THAN ANY OTHER PRESIDENT

A CNN analysis reveals Biden has logged more vacation days in his first year in office than any other President. Let that sink in.

No other President has been on vacation more than Joe Biden.

"While most Presidents have prioritized taking time away from 1600 Pennsylvania Avenue, this is the most time a President has spent away from the White House on personal travel at this point in the presidency in recent history," according to CNN.

Biden has taken 35 trips and spent 108 out of his first 276 days in Office on vacation or working from one of his vacation homes. 69 of those 108 days were spent in

221.   https://www.newsweek.com/jeff-duncan-lets-go-brandon-mask-joe-biden-chant-1642534

Wilmington over 23 visits and 32 were spent at Camp David over 10 visits. [222]

That's 39% of his time in Office so far being spent not being in the office. Does your workplace allow that? I think not.

OCTOBER 25 – BIDEN ADMITS TO CHILDREN THAT HE EVADES REPORTERS

While visiting an elementary school in New Jersey, Biden tells the children, "You know, when you're President — see all these people here, they're with you all the time — they get to ask you all kinds of questions and you try to figure out how you're gonna avoid answering them sometimes."

Well, at least he is honest this once! Biden has been evading questions and reporters all year. [223]

OCTOBER 28 – FEDERAL JUDGE ISSUES RESTRAINING ORDER AGAINST BIDEN

A federal judge issues a temporary restraining order preventing Biden from firing unvaccinated military and federal workers.

Washington, D.C., District Judge Colleen Kollar-Kotelly ordered, "None of the civilian employee plaintiffs will be

222.   https://www.cnn.com/2021/10/23/politics/joe-biden-week-ends-away/index.html

223.   https://www.dailywire.com/news/watch-biden-tells-kids-the-truth-about-him-avoiding-questions-from-the-press

subject to discipline while his or her request for a religious exception is pending." Her ruling added that "active duty military plaintiffs, whose religious exception requests have been denied, will not be disciplined or separated during the pendency of their appeals." [224]

Finally it seems the courts at least are aware of Biden's unconstitutional mandates!

OCTOBER 28 – BIDEN CONFUSES ELECTRIC AND GAS-POWERED CARS

In a speech promoting his "Build Back Better" campaign, Biden claims it is possible to drive across the country in an electric vehicle and only use a tank of gas "figuratively speaking."

"We'll build out the first-ever national network of 500,000 electric vehicle charging stations, all across the country," announced President Biden on Thursday. "So when you buy an electric vehicle — and you get credit for buying it —when you buy an electric vehicle, you can go all the way across America on a single tank of gas, figuratively speaking."

He did not elaborate on what it means to figuratively drive somewhere. [225]

---

224.   https://www.foxnews.com/politics/biden-admin-vaccine-employees-judge-injunction
225.   https://www.youtube.com/watch?v=9oO14JgSKzg

Depending on your route, driving "across the country" can range from 2,500 to 3,500 miles. [226] By comparison, a Nissan Leaf in 2020 averages 226 per battery charge.[227] We assume a single battery charge is equal to "a single tank of gas."

Joe, you'd have to charge up 11 times or more to get "across the country on a single tank of gas" with an electric vehicle. But who's counting?

OCTOBER 29 – BIDEN MEETS WITH THE POPE

Biden meets with Pope Francis in Vatican City. Many Catholics believe that because Biden and the Democratic party seek to expand access to abortion, which the Catholic Church considers a mortal sin, Biden should be denied communion.

After the historic meeting, a reporter asked Biden if the topic of abortion was dealt with at all. "No, it didn't. We just talked about the fact he was happy that I was a good Catholic and I should keep receiving Communion," Biden replied.

Nothing could be further from the truth, Joe. God created humankind in His own image. During our Lord's ministry, we see his tenderness and love for little children. You

---

226. https://traveltips.usatoday.com/long-road-trip-across-america-109310.html
227. https://evcharging.enelx.com/resources/blog/666-how-far-can-electric-cars-go-on-one-charge

cannot advocate for the killing of unborn children and be considered a good Catholic. [228]

OCTOBER 31 – 71% OF AMERICANS BELIEVE THE COUNTRY IS ON THE WRONG TRACK

As we close the month of October, an NBC poll shows 71% of Americans believe the country is on the wrong track.

"When you see a wrong track of 71 percent, it is a flashing red light," said Bill McInturff of Public Opinion Strategies. "These folks are telling us that this is not going well." The poll also revealed that Republicans lead by double digits when it comes to which party Americans believe could do a better job on issues like border security, inflation, crime, national security, and the economy. [229]

Jeff Horwitt, a Democratic pollster with Hart Research Associates, said "Democrats face a country whose opinion of President Biden has turned sharply to the negative since April." [230]

Republicans have a huge opportunity to sweep the country with a Red Wave during 2022 midterm elections. But they must avoid the temptation to compromise our conservative values. Conservatives win elections.

228.   https://time.com/6112047/joe-biden-pope-catholics/
229.   https://www.dailywire.com/news/shock-nbc-poll-shows-americans-have-lost-their-confidence-in-biden-chuck-todd-says
230.   https://www.nbcnews.com/politics/meet-the-press/biden-s-job-rating-sinks-42-percent-nbc-news-poll-n1282781

CHAPTER 11

NOVEMBER 2021:
THE BEGINNING OF THE END?

NOVEMBER 1 – SLEEPY JOE

Washington Post reporter Zac Purser Brown posted a video of Biden falling asleep during the opening speeches at the Glasgow COP26 Climate Change conference.

Maybe the speeches were too boring, or maybe he'd rather be vacationing at his beach house in Delaware. I'm sure the mask he was wearing didn't help.

The video shows him sitting perfectly still with his arms folded and eyes closing before he was awakened by an aide. Biden responded to the aide, rubbed his eyes, folded his hands, and then applauded the speaker at the conclusion of the speech.[231]

This happened at the same event where Obama mixed up being in Scotland for being in the Emerald Isles of Ireland.[232] William Wallace is turning in his grave.

---

231.   https://twitter.com/zachjourno/sta-tus/1455174496164458496
232.   https://www.foxnews.com/politics/obama-mixes-up-scot-land-ireland-cop26-remarks

NOVEMBER 4 – BIDEN CLAIMS FORCED MEDICAL PROCEDURES WILL HELP ECONOMY

Biden's Administration releases a statement about their unconstitutional mandate, saying that there are just too few people voluntarily vaccinated. So what's a Leftist to do? Require people do what they don't want to do, of course!

The statement justifies the mandate by the need to get people back to work. Biden states, "While I would have much preferred that requirements not become necessary, too many people remain unvaccinated for us to get out of this pandemic for good. So I instituted requirements – and they are working."

Biden also claimed that "Vaccination requirements are good for the economy. They not only increase vaccination rates, but they help send people back to work – as many as 5 million American workers. They make our economy more resilient in the face of COVID and keep our businesses open."

Biden reinforces his unconstitutional mandate by saying, "Today, the Labor Department issued its rule requiring COVID-19 vaccinations for companies with 100 or more employees. If you work for one of these companies, you will either need to get vaccinated or test at least weekly. Also today, the Department of Health and Human Services released its rule to ensure that our nation's healthcare workers are vaccinated. No one should be at risk when they seek medical care."[233]

Forcing people to get a medical procedure is not inherently "good for the economy."

But even if it was, the government has no business forcing its citizens to get a medical procedure under threat of losing their job or being subjected to weekly medical tests if they do not. If we allow the government to claim this unconstitutional power, where will it end? Where could it end? The atrocities of previous generations attest to the horrors of where it could end.

I urge Americans to wake up and stand up!

NOVEMBER 4 – FIRST COMPANY SUES BIDEN OVER UNCONSTITUTIONAL VACCINE MANDATE

Prominent conservative media company The Daily Wire becomes one of the first companies to sue Biden over his unconstitutional vaccine mandate. The suit was filed in the U.S. Court of Appeals for the 6th Circuit.

Jeremy Boreing, co-founder of the The Daily Wire, said his company would refuse to comply with Biden's 'tyrannical vaccine mandate.' "President Biden, the federal government, social media, and the establishment media have conspired

233.   https://www.whitehouse.gov/briefing-room/statements-releases/2021/11/04/statement-by-President-joe-biden-on-vaccination-requirements/

to rob Americans of their freedoms in the name of public health," said Boreing. "They have broken faith with the American people through conflicting messaging, false information, and by suppressing data and perspectives with which they disagree."

Biden set a deadline of January 4th for all businesses with at least 100 employees to require proof of vaccination and empowers OSHA as his enforcer.

Many conservative leaders are standing up and announcing legal action against the unconstitutional mandate. Georgia Gov. Brian Kemp (R) announced he would be suing the Biden Administration. Georgia was joined by Alabama, Idaho, Kansas, South Carolina, Utah and West Virginia. [234]

NOVEMBER 6 – FEDERAL COURT STAYS BIDEN'S UNCONSTITUTIONAL MANDATE

A federal court issued a stay against Biden's vaccine mandate for employers with 100 or more employees over legal and constitutional issues.

The ruling from the U.S. Court of Appeals for the Fifth Circuit stated the following:

> Before the court is the petitioners' emergency
> motion to stay enforcement of the Occupational

---

234.   https://thehill.com/homenews/media/580119-ben-shapi-ros-media-company-sues-biden-administration-over-vaccine-man-date

Safety and Health Administration's November 5, 2021 Emergency Temporary Standard (the "Mandate") pending expedited judicial review.

Because the petitions give cause to believe there are grave statutory and constitutional issues with the Mandate, the Mandate is hereby STAYED pending further action by this court.

Some State Officials are Announcing Their plans to take action against the Biden Administration.

"Yesterday, I sued the Biden Admin over its unlawful OSHA vax mandate," Texas Attorney General Ken Paxton said in a statement. "WE WON. Just this morning, citing 'grave statutory and constitutional issues,' the 5th Circuit stayed the mandate. The fight is not over, and I will never stop resisting this Admin's unconstitutional overreach! We will have our day in court to strike down Biden's unconstitutional abuse of authority."

Louisiana Attorney General Jeff Landry wrote on Twitter, "In a major win for the liberty of job creators and their employees, the United States Court of Appeals for the Fifth Circuit just halted the Biden Administration's attempt to force vaccines on businesses with 100 or more workers. The Court's action not only halts Biden from moving forward with his unlawful overreach, but also commands the judicious review we sought. @POTUS will not impose medical procedures on the American people without the checks and balances afforded by our Constitution."

West Virginia Attorney General Patrick Morrisey wrote, "We're diving deeper into how this impacts the entire country, but this is obviously very good news & consistent with our belief that Biden's vaccine mandates are unlawful, unconstitutional & just wrong!" [235]

Whether you agree with the effectiveness of the various COVID vaccines or not, most Americans do not believe Biden's OSHA should force them upon the population.

NOVEMBER 6 – BIDEN IMPLIES AMERICANS AREN'T SMART ENOUGH

Answering a question from a reporter, Biden made remarks that appeared to mock the intelligence of average Americans, implying that they aren't smart enough to understand supply chains.

According to the White House transcript, Biden explains to reporters:

> "COVID has disrupted almost every family one way or another, whether it's wearing a mask or losing a family member. You know, 750,000-plus Americans dead — 750,000."

---

235.   https://www.dailywire.com/news/breaking-feder-al-court-freezes-biden-vaccine-mandate-over-possible-grave-statu-tory-and-constitutional-issues

"And so, people are worried. People are also worried about, you know, coming up — they don't — understandably. 'Why is the price of — of agricultural products — and when I go to the store, why is it higher?'"

"What — like, for example, if I had — if we were all going out and having lunch together and I said, 'Let's ask whoever the — whoever is at the next table, no matter how — what restaurant we're in — have them explain the supply chain to us.' You think they'd understand what we're talking about?"

"They're smart people. But supply chain — 'Well, why is everything backed up?' Well, it's backed up because the people who supply the materials that end up being on our kitchen table or in our — in our fam- — our life — guess what? They're closing those plants because they have COVID."

Can Biden even explain supply chains?

As someone who has been the subject of numerous rumors about the seemingly obvious cognitive decline, you'd think he'd be smart enough not to throw stones while snoozing in a glass house. [236]

---

236.   https://www.dailywire.com/news/biden-accused-of-mocking-americans-intellect-you-think-theyd-understand-what-were-talking-about

NOVEMBER 7 – BIDEN CONTRIBUTES TO GLOBAL EMISSIONS

Biden reportedly loudly passed gas in the presence of Camilla, Duchess of Cornwall, at the Glasgow COP26 Climate Change Conference.

Camilla was apparently shocked by the incident and "hasn't stopped talking about it" since: "It was long and loud and impossible to ignore," an insider told the Daily Mail.[237]

Ironically, he has claimed that reducing methane emissions is one of the most pressing climate issues!

On a more serious note, it does not place America in a good light diplomatically to have a President who cannot behave appropriately or exercise self-control in such important situations.

This happened just after Biden was caught nodding off during a speech a few days earlier.

NOVEMBER 8 – BIDEN ADMINISTRATION IGNORES FEDERAL COURT

The Biden Administration says that businesses should move forward with the unconstitutional vaccine mandate despite the stay in federal court. "People should not wait,"

237.   https://www.dailymail.co.uk/news/article-10172959/Camilla-stopped-talking-hearing-President-break-wind-chat-Cop26-summit.html

White House Deputy Press Secretary Karine Jean-Pierre told reporters during a briefing. "They should continue to move forward and make sure they're getting their workplace vaccinated."

Once again, we see Democrats ignoring the rule of law to get what they want, claiming the ends justify the means. This is very dangerous ground.

The pause was requested by Republican Attorneys General in Texas, Louisiana, Mississippi, South Carolina, and Utah, as well as several private companies.

The Biden Administration asked the court to lift the pause, dismissing the claims of harm as "premature" since the deadlines for vaccination and testing are not until January 4th. The Administration claimed that pausing the requirements "would likely cost dozens or even hundreds of lives per day" as the virus continues to spread.

These are just more scare tactics from the Left designed to take away our civil liberties and force us to comply.[238] If people want to voluntarily accept the vaccination, that is their choice to do so. If someone wants to decline to accept the vaccination, that should also be their choice.

There was a very definite decision made on the coercion or force of medical procedures against one's will at the

---

238.   https://www.cnbc.com/2021/11/08/biden-vaccine-mandate-white-house-tells-business-to-go-ahead-despite-court-pause.html

Nuremburg Trials. Known as the Nuremburg Codes, under article 32 of the 1949 Geneva Convention IV, "medical or scientific experiments not necessitated by the medical treatment of a protected person" are prohibited, with a death penalty levied against those who seek to violate these international laws.

Today, there is a group of over 11,000 medical professionals seeking legal recourse against the CDC, WHO, and the Davos Group for violations against the Nuremburg Codes. [239] Or as they more seriously state: "crimes against humanity."

NOVEMBER 10 – BIDEN ADMITS INFLATION IS A PROBLEM

Biden finally admits that inflation is a problem, apparently being the last person in the country to realize the crisis has everything from groceries to housing to used cars skyrocketing in price.

During an event in Baltimore promoting his infrastructure bill Biden said, "Everything from a gallon of gas to loaf of bread costs more. And it's worrisome, even though wages are going up." [240]

This is a change from a statement he made back in July, where he downplayed inflation. "Some folks have raised

239.   https://rightforliberty.com/nuremburg-trials-2021/
240.   https://www.breitbart.com/politics/2021/11/11/joe-biden-fi-nally-admits-inflation-is-worrisome-three-months-after-dismissing-it-as-temporary/

worries that this could be a sign of persistent inflation. But that's not our view," he said at the White House on July 19. [241]

He was wrong. Inflation reached 6.2% in October, up 0.9% from September — the highest rate since November of 1990.

And are wages going up? Yes, they are, actually, by about 10% (in the service industry).[242] How will businesses adjust to the rising increases in employee wages? You guessed it: by raising their prices.[243]

NOVEMBER 10 – BIDEN MARVELS AT HIGH GAS PRICES

Continuing his speech at the Port of Baltimore, Biden marvels at high gas prices. "Did you ever think you'd be paying this much for a gallon of gas?" Biden said. "In some parts of California, they're paying $4.50 a gallon."

Of course, Biden's insane energy policies are largely to blame for the prices. Suspending gas and oil leases on federal land as well as closing the Keystone XL pipeline reduced the domestic production of oil!

Ignoring the fact that his Administration is to blame, Biden promised the crowd, "Thanks to the steps we're taking, very soon we're going to see the supply chain start catching up

241.   https://www.whitehouse.gov/briefing-room/speeches-re-marks/2021/07/19/remarks-by-President-biden-on-the-economy-3/
242.   https://www.theguardian.com/business/2021/oct/10/us-small-businesses-wages-gene-marks
243.   https://www.theguardian.com/business/2021/oct/10/us-small-businesses-wages-gene-marks

with demand. So not only will we see more record-breaking job growth, we'll see lower prices, faster deliveries as well." [244]

Good, because in February 2017, the average gas price was $2.41 per gallon not today's average of $3.55. [245][246]

NOVEMBER 11 – WHOOPS! ANOTHER RACIST GAFFE

In his Veteran's Day speech, Biden refers to legendary baseball player Satchel Paige. "You know, I've adopted the attitude of the great negro at the time, pitcher in the negro leagues, went on to become a great pitcher in the pros, in the Major League Baseball after Jackie Robison, his name was Satchel Paige," Biden said. [247]

Republicans have been canceled for far less than referring to an African-American by a now-derogatory term.

Perhaps Biden is not racist, after all, but merely forgot that the term has been considered a major faux-pas since the mid-1960's. [248]

244.   https://www.breitbart.com/politics/2021/11/10/joe-biden-marvels-at-4-50-a-gallon-gas-prices-did-you-ever-think-youd-be-paying-this-much/
245.   https://www.eia.gov/todayinenergy/detail.php?id=34392
246.   https://news.yahoo.com/gas-prices-mexi-co-jump-19-185444724.html
247.   https://www.breitbart.com/politics/2021/11/11/watch-joe-biden-says-ive-adopted-attitude-great-negro-during-veterans-day-speech/
248.   https://www.ferris.edu/HTMLS/news/jimcrow/question/2010/october.htm

NOVEMBER 16 – A NEW LOW FOR BIDEN'S APPROVAL RATING

Biden is in real trouble. According to Real Clear Politics, his approval rating hits a new low of 41.9 percent. [249]

Are we surprised? His ridiculous spending has forced the economy into record inflation. His energy policies have sent gas prices soaring. His open border policies have over-whelmed the CBP. Furthermore, promising amnesty and free money will attract millions more to the border. This is unsustainable. The Left was so hellbent on getting rid of Trump, that they rushed to put bumbling Biden in office.

You reap what you sow. [250]

NOVEMBER 19 – BIDEN UNDERMINES THE AMERICAN JUSTICE SYSTEM

The idea that someone is innocent until proven guilty and has a right to a trial in front of a jury of peers is something many Americans are proud is a right guaranteed to us.

Kyle Rittenhouse was found not guilty of murder in connection with his actions in Kenosha, Wisconsin. However, Biden says he is angry and concerned by the verdict of not guilty by a jury of Rittenhouse's peers.

249.   https://www.realclearpolitics.com/epolls/other/President-biden-job-approval-7320.html
250.   https://www.breitbart.com/politics/2021/11/16/nolte-joe-biden-job-approval-hits-two-new-record-lows/

"While the verdict in Kenosha will leave many Americans feeling angry and concerned, myself included, we must acknowledge that the jury has spoken," Biden said in a statement released by the White House. [251]

There are several problems here. First, Biden admitted that he didn't watch the case! Second, why would Biden be concerned unless he didn't believe in one's innocence until proven guilty? Or that we all have a right to a trial by a jury of our peers?

Finally, Biden also accused Rittenhouse of being a white supremacist on a campaign video that he posted on Twitter. Race was clearly not an issue in this case, as those Rittenhouse shot in self-defense were also white. Race is not always at play, and a jury was presented evidence and came to a verdict of not guilty through court proceedings.

Case closed!

NOVEMBER 19 – WHITE HOUSE TWEETS, "LET'S GO BBBRANDON!"

The White House Deputy Press Secretary tweets "Let's go BBBrandon!" in celebration of the passage of the Build Back Better bill in the House and mocking the popular

---

251.   https://www.breitbart.com/politics/2021/11/19/joe-biden-angry-concerned-rittenhouse-jury-verdict-calls-peaceful-protests/

anti-Biden slogan. This pathetic attempt to co-opt the viral chant proves yet again that the Left can't meme. [252]

NOVEMBER 20 – BIDEN SKIPS COGNITIVE TESTING

Results from Biden's physical are released, but notably exclude any cognitive testing, which is arguably what most people who have observed Biden over the past year are most interested in seeing.

CNN Chief Medical Correspondent Sanjay Gupta was asked if Biden was tested for anything "that measured mental acuity" like former President Donald Trump.

> "It doesn't seem like it. I read pretty carefully through the doctor's report, and there was, they mentioned neurological exam, but that was more in terms of testing motor strength and sensation and things like that. President Trump had something known as the Montreal cognitive assessment. It's sort of a screening test for dementia. And, you know, that there was no mention of that sort of thing here. It is a constant point of discussion. I can tell you within the geriatrics community, I wrote this book last year about brain health, and one of the things that kept coming up was, should sort of these types of screening tests, cognitive screening tests, be more commonly done? And there's many in that community who believe starting at age 65, there should be some sort of screening that's done. Dr.

252.   https://twitter.com/AndrewJBates46/status/1461707867413745665

Ronald Peterson, who runs the Alzheimer's clinic at Mayo has been somebody who talked about that. But as far as we know, for President Biden, we didn't see any kind of tests like that performed."

Despite the lack of cognitive testing, Kevin O'Connor, D.O., FAAFP who serves as the physician to the president, claimed that Joe Biden "remains fit for duty, and fully executes all of his responsibilities without any exemptions or accommodations." [253]

I'm not sure the rest of the country agrees.

NOVEMBER 22 – DOUBLE-STANDARD BIDEN

After Kyle Rittenhouse acted in self-defense in Waukesha, Wisconsin, Biden was quick to defame him as a white supremacist. This is after Kyle was tried extensively and thoroughly in a court of law and acquitted by a jury of his peers.

But after a horrific act of violence which killed 5 people and injured 40 more when a man drove his SUV into a Christmas parade crowd, Biden tried to dispel the outrage with the phrase "we don't have all the facts yet."

"Before I begin, I want to comment on the tragedy that occurred last night during the holiday parade in Wisconsin.

253.   https://www.dailywire.com/news/bidens-physical-reveals-multiple-health-issues-does-not-appear-to-have-gotten-cognitive-test-reports

While we don't have all the facts and details yet, we know this morning that five families in Waukesha are facing fresh grief, a life without a loved one. At least 40 Americans are suffering from injuries, some of them in critical condition, and an entire community is struggling, struggling to cope with the horrific act of violence. Last night, people of Waukesha were gathered to celebrate the start of a season of hope and togetherness and thanksgiving," Biden said. [254]

The suspect, Darrell Brooks, Jr., is a Black man with a criminal record. Waukesha's population is 98% white. [255] I am not saying this was a racially motivated crime, because only God knows the motives of the heart. However, for Biden to have such a blatant double standard in this case is nauseating.

BNOVEMBER 22 – BIDEN HIDES BEHIND ELEVATOR MUSIC

Biden has faced much criticism for refusing to answer questions from reporters regarding the many crises his Administration is presiding over. As his first year in office draws to a close, he is taking fewer and fewer questions.

To try to improve the optics, his team tried something never done before. They played elevator music to drown out the reporters as Biden exited the fake White House set after

254. https://www.dailywire.com/news/biden-on-waukesha-trage-dy-we-dont-have-all-the-facts-and-details-yet
255. https://www.npr.org/2021/11/23/1058241281/the-suspect-in-the-wis-christmas-parade-attack-has-a-previous-criminal-record

ignoring the press. That's right—the fake White House with digital windowpanes.

He campaigned from his basement, spends more time on vacation than any other President, and holds his rare press conferences from a fake White House.

He did end on a positive note, "I know, for a lot of Americans, things are still very hard — very hard," he said. "But if we look at the facts — all the facts — you can only come to one conclusion: We have made enormous progress in this country."

But does anyone really believe this? [256]

NOVEMBER 22 – BIDEN CONFIRMS HE WILL RUN AGAIN IN 2024

White House Press Secretary confirms that Joe Biden will be running for re-election in 2024. "That's his intention," Psaki told reporters aboard Air Force One. [257] Dear God, please, no!

When Biden was asked in March if he will run again for the Presidency, he responded in the affirmative. "The answer is yes, my plan is to run for reelection," Biden said. "That's my expectation."

256.   https://www.breitbart.com/politics/2021/11/22/staff-plays-music-joe-biden-exits-fake-white-house-set-no-questions/
257.   https://www.theguardian.com/us-news/2021/nov/21/joe-biden-2024-reportedly-telling-allies-running-for-President

Biden was already the oldest candidate to assume the office of President. He will be two weeks shy of his 82nd birthday on November 5, 2024. Trump, who has yet to formally announce his campaign, will be 78 on election day. [258]

One imagines that Republican Presidential hopefuls are excited by this possibility. According to a Hill-HarrisX Poll, nearly two-thirds of voters do not want him to run. Biden has failed at leading our country, leaving us with multiple crises. [259]

NOVEMBER 24 – "BARE SHELVES BIDEN" STRIKES AGAIN

Ahead of Thanksgiving, Biden tweeted that grocery stores were stocked with plenty of food. "For all those concerns a few weeks ago that there would not be ample food available for Thanksgiving, families can rest easy today. Grocery stores are well-stocked with turkey and everything else you need." Biden claimed. [260]

At the same time, many grocery stores rationed food items to ensure that shelves weren't completely wiped out. Publix Supermarkets warned customers to expect food shortages in all 1,280 stores across the southeast.

258.   https://www.politico.com/news/2021/03/25/biden-run-reelection-2024-478008
259.   https://www.breitbart.com/politics/2021/11/16/poll-nearly-2-3-of-voters-want-joe-biden-to-step-aside-let-another-candidate-run-in-2024/
260.   https://twitter.com/POTUS/status/1463568779288449029

According to the Orlando Sentinel, the list of rationed items includes the following:[261]

- Canned cranberry sauce
- Jarred gravy
- Canned pie filling
- Canola and vegetable oil
- Cream cheese
- Bacon
- Rolled breakfast sausage
- Paper napkins
- Disposable plates, cups and cutlery
- Bath tissue
- Refrigerated snacks (Lunchables-type items)
- Sports drinks
- Aseptic-type juices (Capri Sun)
- Canned cat food (variety packs)
- Refrigerated pet food

Winn-Dixie rationed turkeys, the price of which has risen 24% since 2020.[262]

261.   https://www.orlandosentinel.com/business/os-bz-pub-lix-thanksgiving-limits-20211122-dx72yaz2jrblhexan4c3kwqib4-story.html
262.   https://www.breitbart.com/economy/2021/11/24/joe-biden-claims-shelves-are-well-stocked-as-grocers-ration-food/

NOVEMBER 24 – VACCINATIONS DID NOT DECREASE FATALITIES

The New York Times reports that more people have died in 2021 of COVID than in 2020, despite the widespread availability of vaccines. The Times cited the Centers for Disease Control and Prevention's (CDC) Tuesday figures, which reported 386,233 COVID related fatalities for 2021.

In all of 2020, there were 385,343 fatalities recorded nationally. The 2021 figure is only expected to rise, since there is still over one month left in the year. [263]

The Times also blamed "lower-than-needed vaccination rates" and the relaxing of everyday precautions such as masking and social distancing. But this doesn't add up when you look at the facts. States that brought back mask mandates like Illinois, Michigan, New York, and Pennsylvania saw an uptick in cases, whereas Florida is showing the lowest per capita rate in the nation despite the early avoidance of mandates.

During the second Presidential debate, Biden said "220,000 Americans dead. If you hear nothing else I say tonight, hear this — anyone who is responsible for that many deaths should not remain as President of the United States of America." [264]

263.   https://www.nytimes.com/live/2021/11/24/world/covid-vac-
cine-boosters-mandates#united-states-death-toll-covid
264.   https://www.breitbart.com/politics/2021/11/24/new-york-
times-admits-more-coronavirus-deaths-under-joe-biden-despite-

Well, I guess it's time for Biden to resign!

NOVEMBER 26 – THE RISE OF OMICRON AND MORE HYPOCRISY FROM BIDE

Biden restricts travel from several African nations after a new COVID variant is discovered there. But when Trump enacted travel restrictions to attempt to control the spread of COVID, Biden called that xenophobic and racist!

On February 1, 2020, Biden tweeted, "We are in the midst of a crisis with the coronavirus. We need to lead the way with science — not Donald Trump's record of hysteria, xenophobia, and fear-mongering. He is the worst possible person to lead our country through a global health emergency." [265]

NOVEMBER 27 – MASKS FOR THEE, BUT NOT FOR ME!

Biden claims that masks are important to stop the spread of Omicron. So why is he continually photographed without a mask? The latest incident was in a store that had a "mask required" sign posted on the door.

"The President was seen inside Murray's Toggery Shop on the island of Nantucket Saturday with his mask around his neck and not covering his mouth despite a visible sign outside the door instructing patrons to wear a mask,"

vaccines/
265.   https://twitter.com/JoeBiden/status/1223727977361338370

Fox News reported. "Nantucket, where Biden is spending his Thanksgiving holiday, re-instituted an indoor mask mandate earlier this month."[266]

Once again, the rhetoric from the mouth and the actions from the Left are completely opposite.

NOVEMBER 28 – BIDEN IS NOT AS UNPOPULAR AS HARRIS

Biden's approval ratings may be tanking, but he can take comfort in the fact that at least he is not as unpopular as his Vice President!

A poll reveals only 13% of Democrats would support Kamala Harris if she ran for President in 2024. Michelle Obama came in 2nd place at 10%. Neither got most of the support. 36% said they were unsure if Biden doesn't run. 13% said they would choose someone not on the list of options.

The Hill reported on its Hill-HarrisX poll, which surveyed 939 registered Democrat voters from November 18 to November 19, said: "All other candidates listed received 5 percent or less support, with most voters surveyed still unsure of who they would back if Biden chose not run. Other candidates in the poll included 2020 Presidential hopefuls Bernie Sanders, Elizabeth Warren, Cory Booker, Michael Bloomberg, Andrew Yang and Pete Buttigieg."

---

266. https://www.foxnews.com/politics/biden-spotted-in-nantucket-shopping-indoors-without-a-mask-despite-sign-mandating-them

The margin of error is plus or minus 3.2 percentage points.[267]

NOVEMBER 30 – MASKS FOR THEE, BUT NOT FOR ME!

At a Christmas event, children of military service members were forced to wear masks and socially distance, but First Lady Jill Biden went mask-less.

The book she read, "Don't Forget, God Bless our Troops," happened to be one she wrote.[268] I haven't read her book, but the title sounds both conservative and patriotic.

While the message may be heart-warming, what message are the kids really hearing? Their faces are mandatorily covered, and they are seated 6-feet apart while listening to a woman without a mask.

Does any of this make sense?

NOVEMBER 30 – FEDERAL JUDGE STOPS BIDEN'S MANDATE IN 3 STATES

A federal judge in Kentucky rules that Biden cannot impose his vaccine mandate on Federal contractors in Kentucky, Ohio, and Tennessee.

---

267.   https://thehill.com/hilltv/what-americas-thinking/583018-poll-harris-michelle-obama-lead-for-2024-if-biden-doesnt-run
268.   https://www.breitbart.com/politics/2021/11/30/jill-biden-goes-maskless-as-children-forced-to-wear-masks-at-the-white-house-for-christmas-event/

The Lexington Herald Leader reported: "U.S. District Judge Gregory F. Van Tatenhove, who serves the Eastern District of Kentucky, issued the opinion and order Tuesday afternoon. It came in response to a challenge from Kentucky Attorney General Daniel Cameron, who joined many other state attorneys general in challenging the mandate."

"The question presented here is narrow," Van Tatenhove said. "Can the President use congressionally delegated authority to manage the federal procurement of goods and services to impose vaccines on the employees of federal contractors and subcontractors? In all likelihood, the answer to that question is no."

"These questions will not be finally resolved in the shadows. Instead, the consideration will continue with the benefit of full briefing and appellate review. But right now, the enforcement of the contract provisions in this case must be paused," Van Tatenhove ruled.

Attorney General Daniel Cameron celebrated the ruling, "This is a significant ruling because it gives immediate relief from the federal government's vaccine requirement to Kentuckians who either contract with the federal government or work for a federal contractor." [269]

---

269.   https://www.kentucky.com/news/politics-government/article256230412.html

NOVEMBER 30 – FEDERAL JUDGE STOPS BIDEN'S MANDATE IN ANOTHER 10 STATES

A Federal judge in Missouri rules that Biden cannot impose his vaccine mandate on health care workers in 10 states. The preliminary injunction by St. Louis-based U.S. District Judge Matthew Schelp applies to Alaska, Arkansas, Iowa, Kansas, Missouri, Nebraska, New Hampshire, North Dakota, South Dakota and Wyoming. These states, which united for the lawsuit, have either a Republican attorney general or governor.

Similar lawsuits are pending in other states. This is one of many legal setbacks for the Biden Administration's plan to force medical procedures on the American people.[270]

---

270.   https://news.yahoo.com/biden-vaccine-rule-health-work-ers-184137096.html

CHAPTER 12

DECEMBER 2021:
EVEN CHINA MOCKS BIDEN

DECEMBER 7 – GEORGIA V. BIDEN. BIDEN LOSES.

U.S. District Court Judge R. Stan Baker of the Southern District of Georgia blocked Biden's vaccine mandate for federal contractors in all 50 states. The mandate would have affected about 25% of the United States workforce. Baker's ruling follows a Kentucky Federal Judge's preliminary injunction in a lawsuit involving Kentucky, Tennessee, and Ohio just last week.

Idaho Gov. Brad Little cheered Tuesday's ruling in a statement, "Yet another one of President Biden's vaccine mandates have been temporarily shut down because the states—including Idaho—took a stand against his unprecedented government overreach into Americans' lives and businesses," Little said. "All three mandates are now completely stalled. We will continue to press forward in our fight against the federal government's bad policies."

Associated Builders and Contractors, which joined in the seven-state suit, stated: "This is a big win in removing compliance hurdles for the construction industry, which is facing economic challenges, such as a workforce shortage of 430,000, rising materials prices, and supply chain issues." [271]

DECEMBER 7 – CHINA MOCKS BIDEN AND HIS DIPLOMATIC BOYCOTT

Biden announces a "diplomatic boycott" of the Beijing 2022 Winter Olympics over human rights abuses. White House Press Secretary Jen Psaki claimed, "Not sending a U.S. delegation sends a clear message that we cannot conduct ourselves with business as usual. We feel this sends a clear message."

US athletes would compete as usual, but government officials would not attend.

China mocked Biden's boycott, saying that the officials weren't invited anyway and are not participating in the Olympics. Chen Weihua, an editor with the China Daily, repeatedly responded to news of the diplomatic "boycott" by stating, "You're not invited and not welcome, Mr. Biden," Chen wrote. "Hope you will live long enough to see China boycotting Los Angeles Summer Games in 2028."

Chinese Ministry spokesman Zhao Lijian said, "U.S. politicians keep hyping a 'diplomatic boycott' without even being invited to the Games. This wishful thinking and pure grandstanding is aimed at political manipulation. It is a

271.   https://news.bloomberglaw.com/daily-labor-report/
biden-vaccine-mandate-for-federal-contractors-blocked-nationwide

grave travesty of the spirit of the Olympic Charter, a blatant political provocation and a serious affront to the 1.4 billion Chinese people." [272]

DECEMBER 9 – ONLY 22% OF AMERICANS SUPPORT A BIDEN RUN IN 2024

A new I&I/TIPP Poll of Americans' preference for the 2024 Democratic Presidential ballot reveals that only 22% of Americans want Biden to run for President in 2024, but only 12% want Harris to run. There is also no clear frontrunner Democrat to run in his place. [273]

"It's undeniable. Joe Biden is hurting in the polls right now and it's due to a number of factors," Erin O'Brien, associate professor of political science at UMass Boston, told the Boston Herald. [274]

DECEMBER 10 – IGNORANCE IS BLISS

Biden tells Jimmy Fallon that he doesn't pay attention to his approval rating anymore. With an approval rating as low as Biden's, ignorance must be bliss!

272.   https://www.breitbart.com/asia/2021/12/07/youre-not-invit-ed-china-laughs-off-joe-bidens-olympics-half-measure/

273.   https://tippinsights.com/i-i-tipp-poll-stunner-just-22-of-ameri-cans-want-joe-biden-to-run-for-President-again/

274.   https://www.bostonherald.com/2021/12/07/biden-re-elec-

Fallon asked Biden, "How much do you pay attention to approval ratings?" Biden replied, "Well, not anymore," prompting laughter from Fallon and the audience.

Biden shook it off saying, "I paid attention when they were in the mid-60s. Now it's in the mid-40s; I don't pay attention anymore."

Blindly supporting Biden, Fallon encouraged him saying, "You came in, you came in hot, you got to medium, and now you're at a low, but you've just got to keep your head down, right, and doing the right thing?"

Biden explained his plummeting approval ratings by saying, "Well look, here's the deal, I think that its — we've been in [office] less than a year, a lot has happened, and look, people are afraid, people are worried. And people are getting so much inaccurate information to them, I don't mean about me, but about their situation. So they're, you know, they're being told that, you know, that Armageddon's on the way. The truth is the economy's grown more than it has [at] any time in close to 60 years, the unemployment rate is down to 4.2%, and it's going to go lower, in my view."

Admitting to skyrocketing inflation, Biden said, "We do have inflation on things that in fact matter to people's lives. When you show up at a gas station and it's $3.50 at your pump, although now that I took 50 million barrels out of the

[Strategic Petroleum Reserve], the gasoline is down below $3.00 in many places, it's gonna come down, it's gonna move. In the meantime, people are worried. ... There's a lot of anxiety." [275]

Yes, Mr. Biden, there is serious anxiety. America is looking for you to pivot and do the right thing before it is too late. But you're goofing around, snoozing, and muttering under your breath incoherently.

DECEMBER 13 – BIDEN WILLING TO LOSE HIS PRESIDENCY

Biden says he'd be willing to lose the Presidency over how he handled Afghanistan.

During an interview with Biden, CBS News correspondent Rita Braver asked him, "This has been a hard year. I mean, we're in the middle of a pandemic. You know that various things that you've done have gotten a lot of criticism. You've had a hard time getting the other side to work with you ... don't you ever feel discouraged about this?"

"No," Biden answered.

Braver followed up by asking, "And doesn't that criticism get to you? And how does Dr. B help you through that?" Biden responded, "Well, you know, I guess it should get to me more. But look: one of the things we did decide, and I mean this, my word as a Biden, I know what I'm willing to lose

275.   https://www.dailywire.com/news/biden-on-jimmy-fallon-i-dont-pay-attention-to-approval-ratings-anymore

over. If we walk away from the middle class, if we walk away from trying to unify people, if we start to engage in the same kind of politics that the last four years has done? I'm willing to lose over that."

Taken aback, Braver asked Biden to clarify, "You mean, you're willing to lose your Presidency?"

Biden fired back, "My Presidency, that's right. Because I'm gonna stick with it. There's certain things that are just, like for example Afghanistan. Well, I've been against that war in Afghanistan from the very beginning. We were spending $300 million a week in Afghanistan, over 20 years. Now, everybody says, 'You could have gotten out without anybody being hurt.' No one's come up with a way to ever indicate to me how that happens. ... And so, there are certain things that are just so important." [276]

At the time I was writing this book, Trump came out swinging against Biden's handling of Afghanistan in an interview with NewsMax. "I think the withdrawal from Afghanistan was so bad on so many fronts. Number one: The way it was done. I was the one who was going to get out. But we were going to get out with strength and dignity. To this day many Americans are left behind."

"Nobody even knows what happened," said Trump, "But you had 13 killed and many, many wounded of our military

276.   https://www.dailywire.com/news/biden-brags-hed-be-will-ing-to-lose-presidency-over-disastrous-afghanistan-withdrawal

and other people. We took our military out first. It was absolutely ridiculous. Then, of course, you had $85 billion worth of equipment -- 70,000 trucks, 700,000 machine guns and rifles [left behind]. ... One of the most incredible, stupid deals, that I've ever heard of." [277]

This is clearly one of the worst executed military withdrawals in our nation's history—a failure of epic proportions. Countless lives affected by the absolute bungling at the hands of Biden and his Administration

DECEMBER 16 – WINTER IS COMING

Biden tries to frighten Americans into getting vaccinated and warns of winter of severe sickness and death from the Omicron variant.

During a COVID-19 briefing at the White House, Biden scolded the American people through the press, "I want to send a direct message to the American people: Due to the steps we've taken, Omicron has not yet spread as fast as it would've otherwise done and as is happening in Europe. But it's here now, and it's spreading, and it's going to increase. For unvaccinated, we are looking at a winter of severe illness and death — if you're unvaccinated — for themselves, their families, and the hospitals they'll soon overwhelm. But there's good news: If you're vaccinated and

277.   https://www.newsmax.com/newsfront/trump-biden-border-economy/2022/02/04/id/1055525/?dkt_nbr=6F1212ecst8a

you had your booster shot, you're protected from severe illness and death — period." [278]

Omicron is a much less severe form of the virus, which many experience as equivalent to a cold or mild flu, and which seems to be much less likely to kill than Delta or the original Covid-19 strain.

DECEMBER 17 – PRESIDENT HARRIS?

While delivering the commencement address at South Carolina State University, Biden referred to Vice President Kamala Harris as "President Harris" – again.

"All kidding aside, of course President Harris is a proud Howard alum — she might have something to say about Delaware State," Biden said.

Biden has made this same gaffe several times at this point. Incidentally, polls indicate that Harris would be even less popular as President than Joe Biden currently is rated.[279]

DECEMBER 17 – LIBERAL COURT SIDES WITH BIDEN

U.S. Appeals Court for the Sixth Circuit rules 2-1 that Biden's vaccine mandate for employers with more than

---

278.   https://www.whitehouse.gov/briefing-room/speeches-re-marks/2021/12/16/remarks-by-President-biden-after-meeting-with-members-of-the-covid-19-response-team/
279.   https://www.dailywire.com/news/President-harris-bidens-gaffe-filled-commencement-speech-raises-eyebrows

100 employees can go forward despite a number of Judges ruling it is unconstitutional.

Obama appointee, Judge Jane Branstetter Stranch, spoke for the majority: "Recognizing that the "old normal" is not going to return, employers and employees have sought new models for a workplace that will protect the safety and health of employees who earn their living there. In need of guidance on how to protect their employees from COVID-19 transmission while reopening business, employers turned to the Occupational Safety and Health Administration (OSHA or the Agency), the federal agency tasked with assuring a safe and healthful workplace." [280]

One should not be surprised that a court with a liberal majority would support Biden's mandate. This is another reminder that elections matter because Presidents appoint Federal Judges.

DECEMBER 17 – BIDEN GIVES "POSTHUMOUS" AWARD TO LIVING HERO

The Biden Administration announces a posthumous award of the Medal of Honor for conspicuous gallantry at the risk of his life and above the call of duty to Staff Sargant Earl Plumlee –– who was very much alive and standing right next to Biden.

---

280.   https://www.foley.com/en/insights/publications/2022/01/get-your-popcorn-supreme-court-is-back-in-session

Marine Lt. Col. William Kerrigan, military aide to Biden said, "Attention to orders. The President of the United States of America, authorized by act of Congress March 3, 1863, has posthumously awarded in the name of Congress the Medal of Honor to Staff Sgt. Earl D. Plumlee, United States Army, for conspicuous gallantry at the risk of his life and above and beyond the call of duty." [281]

Regardless of what appears to be a clerical mistake, Staff Sergeant Earl D. Plumlee is clearly a hero and worthy of our recognition.

The White House issued the following statement about Plumlee's heroism in the U.S. War in Afghanistan:

> "Master Sergeant Earl D. Plumlee will receive the Medal of Honor for his acts of gallantry and intre-pidity above and beyond the call of duty on August 28th, 2013, while serving as a Weapons Sergeant, C Company, 4th Battalion, 1st Special Forces Group (Airborne), in support of Operation Enduring Freedom in Afghanistan.
>
> While deployed to Afghanistan, then-Staff Sergeant Plumlee instantly responded to a complex enemy attack that began with a massive explosion that tore a sixty-foot breach in the base's perimeter wall. Ten insurgents wearing Afghan National Army uniforms and suicide vests poured through the

281.   https://www.dailywire.com/news/watch-biden-admin-an-nounces-posthumous-medal-of-honor-for-living-recipient-standing-in-room

breach. Staff Sergeant Plumlee and five Special Operations members, intent upon defending the base, mounted two vehicles and raced toward the site of the detonation. The vehicles, now no longer under cover, came under effective enemy fire from the front and right. Using his body to shield the driver from enemy fire, he instinctively reacted, exiting the vehicle while simultaneously drawing his pistol and engaging an insurgent to the vehicle's right. Without cover and with complete disregard for his own safety, he advanced on the superior enemy force engaging multiple insurgents with only his pistol. Upon reaching cover, he killed two insurgents, one with a well-placed grenade and the other by detonating the insurgent's suicide vest using precision sniper fire. Again disregarding his own safety, he left cover and advanced alone against the superior enemy force engaging several combatants at close range, including an insurgent whose suicide vest exploded a mere seven meters from his position. Undeterred and resolute, he joined a small group of American and Polish Soldiers, who moved from cover to counter-attack the infiltrators. As the force advanced, he engaged an insurgent to his front left. The wounded insurgent threw a grenade before detonating his suicide vest. Staff Sergeant Plumlee then swung around and engaged another insurgent who charged the group from the rear. The insurgent detonated his suicide vest, mortally wounding a U.S. Soldier. Staff Sergeant Plumlee, with complete disregard for his own safety, ran to the wounded Soldier, carried him to safety, and rendered first aid. He then organized three Polish Soldiers for defense, methodically cleared the area, remained in a security posture, and continued to scan for any remaining threats.

Master Sergeant Plumlee enlisted in the Oklahoma Army National Guard in October 1998. Following his high school graduation in May 2000, he was released from the Oklahoma Army National Guard to join the U.S. Marine Corps. He served in the Marine Corps and Marine Corps Reserve from May 2000 to December 2008. Following his separation from the Marine Corps Reserve, Master Sergeant Plumlee enlisted in the U.S. Army on February 5th, 2009. He has numerous overseas deployments to include Iraq and Afghanistan and is currently serving as a Senior Weapons Sergeant with Headquarters and Head-quarters Company, 1st Special Forces Group at Fort Lewis, Washington." [282]

Thank you, Staff Sergeant Plumlee, for your great service to this nation.

If President Trump was in office, we would have much more to show for the past twenty years, and I doubt he would have botched up your honors ceremony.

---

282.   https://www.whitehouse.gov/briefing-room/statements-re-leases/2021/12/10/President-joseph-r-biden-jr-to-award-medal-of-honor/

DECEMBER 21 – BIDEN COUGHS DURING COVID-19 PRESS CONFERENCE

Biden gives a press conference about COVID-19 booster shots and has a noticeable cough. "There are some parts of this country where people are very eager to get their booster where it's harder to get an appointment," pausing briefly to cough into his hand. "Excuse me. Starting this week I'll be deploying hundreds more vaccinators and more sites to help get the booster shots in people's arms. I've ordered FEMA, the Federal Emergency Management Agency, to stand up new pop-up vaccination clinics all across the country, where you can get that booster shot. We've opened –" Biden coughed again into his hand again before continuing, "Excuse me. We've opened FEMA vaccination sites in Washington state and New Mexico recently as cases have increased." [283]

The coughing did not go unnoticed and was talked about heavily on Twitter, wondering if Biden had "COVID cough."

Darlene Superville, White House Reporter for the Associated Press, quickly tweeted, "@PressSec says Biden is asymptomatic after his close contact last week with a staffer who later tested positive for COVID-19. He's asymptomatic. I spent several hours with him this morning and he is feeling great."[284]

---

283.   https://www.dailywire.com/news/biden-coughs-through-his-covid-19-press-conference

284.   https://twitter.com/dsupervilleap/sta-

DECEMBER 24 – BIDEN SAYS, "LET'S GO, BRANDON!"

Hold on folks, America gets an early Christmas present with this one! As Biden took calls from the NORAD Santa program, a caller ended his call with the slogan, "Let's Go, Brandon!"

Biden happily chortled in response, "Let's go, Brandon, I agree," apparently still not understanding the slogan stands in for, "F—k Joe Biden." [285]

The caller was Jared Schmeck, 35, a father of four who works for an electric company and is a former Medford police officer. "I have nothing against Mr. Biden, but I am frustrated because I think he can be doing a better job," Jared told The Oregonian. "I mean no disrespect to him." Schmeck describes himself as a free-thinking American.[286]

It certainly was a shocking thing to say to a sitting U.S. President. While lawful under the First Amendment, it perhaps lacked decorum. Sadly, Shmeck has received numerous threats from Left-wing whackos for his farewell comment to Biden.

---

tus/1473373121570910220
285.   https://www.dailywire.com/news/biden-mocked-online-after-agreeing-with-lets-go-brandon-he-is-more-clueless-than-we-even-thought
286.   https://www.oregonlive.com/nation/2021/12/oregon-father-of-four-who-told-President-biden-lets-go-brandon-on-christmas-eve-call-said-he-meant-it-in-jest.html

DECEMBER 25 – SANTA FORGETS ONE OF THE BIDEN'S GRANDCHILDREN

The White House decorated for Christmas, in a garish and unusual fashion unlike the classy displays presented by our former First Lady, Melania.

Perhaps most disturbing is the array of stockings for each of the Biden grandchildren that failed to include Hunter Biden's daughter, Navy![287] How sad. It breaks my heart.

When this was pointed out, rather than add the missing stocking, the Bidens simply removed all of the stockings!

As a grandfather, this seems highly strange to me. How can you exclude one of your grandchildren, particularly at Christmas!

DECEMBER 27 – BIDEN GIVES UP ON FIGHT AGAINST COVID?

In 2020, Biden promised, "I'm going to shut down the virus," but now he back-pedals: "There is no Federal solution."

Arkansas Governor Asa Hutchinson (R), chairman of the National Governors Association, spoke about challenges his state is experiencing in their response to the pandemic:

---

287.   https://nypost.com/2021/12/01/bidens-stocking-display-excludes-hunters-daughter-born-out-of-wedlock/

"And so one word of concern or encouragement for your team is that as you look towards federal solutions that will help alleviate the challenge, make sure that we do not let federal solution stand in the way of state solutions. And the production of 500 million rapid tests that will be distributed by the federal government is great. But obviously that dries up the supply chain for the solutions that we might offer as governor."

Biden responded, "Look, there is no Federal solution. This gets solved at the state level."[288]

As the saying goes, even a broken clock is right twice a day. You are right, Mr. Biden. States can handle this much better than the federal government. Some states handle it better than others as have we clearly seen over the past two years. Florida, for example.

DECEMBER 28 – GOVERNOR KRISTI NOEM HOLDS BIDEN ACCOUNTABLE

South Dakota Governor Kristi Noem asks Biden to rescind his vaccine mandate on companies with more than 100 people after his claim yesterday that "There is no Federal solution" to the fight against COVID.

> "After a year, we finally agree @potus. The federal government isn't the solution. That's why from

---

288.   https://www.dailywire.com/news/after-promising-to-shut-down-the-virus-biden-now-claims-there-is-no-federal-solution

the start, SD took a different approach by trusting our citizens to be responsible and make the right decisions for themselves & their families. Now rescind all the federal mandates," Noem said on Twitter. [289]

Noem had previously criticized Biden over his frightening comments just before Christmas where he told unvaccinated Americans they would be "looking at a winter of severe illness and death for yourselves, your families, and the hospitals you may soon overwhelm."

"Severe illness and death? Really Mr. President? America needs hope and leadership from Biden. Not fear and dire predictions - America has met every challenge head on and with optimism for generations. Our country will get through this together," Noem posted on Twitter. [290]

DECEMBER 28 – COVID DEATHS UNDER BIDEN SURPASS THOSE UNDER TRUMP

The US has the most new COVID-19 cases in one day— 150,000—despite Biden's incessant pushing of vaccines, boosters, and lecturing of Americans to don face masks.

"The U.S. logged its highest single-day total of new Covid-19 cases on Tuesday, with 441,278 infections surpassing the

289.   https://twitter.com/KristiNoem/status/1475833822444982279
290.   https://twitter.com/KristiNoem/status/1473016740011560964

previous daily record by close to 150,000. The Centers for Disease Control and Prevention's tally represents a grim new milestone in the coronavirus pandemic and comes as the Omicron strain has quickly taken hold throughout the U.S., leading to long lines at testing sites and sold-out rapid tests at many stores." [291]

During his campaign, Biden repeatedly pledged that he would "shut down the virus." The CDC reported back in January that on January 20, 2021, at 1:16PM, there were 400,306 deaths recorded in the U.S. from the coronavirus.

Biden officially became President of the United States at noon on that day. Since then, the number of people who have died from coronavirus under Biden's watch is now greater than 400,306. [292]

DECEMBER 29 – BIZARRE BIDEN CLAIM

Biden bizarrely claims that 2021 has been the strongest first year economically of any President in 50 years—despite runaway inflation and multiple crises!

"We're ending 2021 with what one analyst described as the strongest first-year economic track record of any President

---

291.   https://www.politico.com/news/2021/12/28/us-new-daily-high-covid-526223

292.   https://web.archive.org/web/20210121045133/https://covid.cdc.gov/covid-data-tracker/#cases_casesper100klast7days

in the last 50 years," Biden wrote on Twitter. "Let's keep the progress going." [293]

Who was the analyst, Joe? I guess if you tell a lie long enough and hard enough, people will believe it. It's hard to imagine how Biden can even say this when all Americans are feeling the effects of skyrocketing inflation and soaring gas prices.

President Trump was widely mocked by Democrats for his self-congratulatory statements, but at least most of them were based in some sort of reality.

And what "one analyst" does he refer to? I'd like to interview them and find out where their economics degree came from, because last time I checked the rampant inflation hikes we've experienced is not a good track record.

DECEMBER 29 – USELESS MASKS

Joe and Jill Biden photographed walking down a Delaware beach wearing masks, despite being outside, triple-vaccinated, and no one else nearby.

"The President, 79, even continued to wear his mask after the First Lady, 70, took hers off. It's not clear who Biden believed he was protecting or who he felt he needed protection from as the only other people on the beach, the

293.　https://www.dailywire.com/news/biden-lauds-strongest-first-year-economic-track-record-of-any-President-in-50-years-in-bizarre-tweet-despite-economic-crises

Secret Service, didn't come within 10 yards," The Daily Mail reported. [294]

The latest guidance from the Centers for Disease Control (CDC) states, "In general, you do not need to wear a mask in outdoor settings. In areas with high numbers of COVID-19 cases, consider wearing a mask in crowded outdoor settings and for activities with close contact with others who are not fully vaccinated." [295]

Since none of the CDC's scenarios applied here, perhaps the Bidens were wearing their masks purely for the sake of photographers.

294.   https://www.dailymail.co.uk/news/article-10351263/Joe-Biden-says-bit-progress-home-testing-kits-private-calls-Tuesday.html
295.   https://www.cdc.gov/coronavirus/2019-ncov/vaccines/stay-up-to-date.html?CDC_AA_refVal=https%3A%2F%2Fwww.cdc.gov%2Fcoronavirus%2F2019-ncov%2Fvaccines%2Ffully-vaccinated.html

EPILOGUE

As I said in the introduction, the purpose of this book is to validate your frustration with the incompetent Biden-Harris Administration by documenting the faux pas, fiascos, and failures of their first year in power.

More could have been written, but I wanted to keep the size of this book to a manageable level. This is, after all, the first volume.

I also have a higher purpose for writing this book. It was not simply to gripe and complain about what is going on in our country. Nor is it meant to create yet another conservative echo-chamber.

Identifying the problem is the first step toward developing a solution. The temporary solution is to win the mid-terms in 2022 and the White House in 2024.

But even the next two election cycles are just that. Cycles. Even if we win those elections, will Conservatives continue to win long-term?

We know the Left will continue their attack on American values and our way of life until there is nothing left of our beloved country. During the proofreading process, my wife made the comment that this book is depressing.

It reminded me that there is a lasting and long-term solution that I must share with you now.

We must first recognize that America's problems are spiritual rather than merely political. As the late Andrew Breitbart said, politics are downstream of culture. I will take it back one step and suggest that culture is downstream of our faith.

A secular religion creates a secular culture, which creates secular politics. A Christian faith creates a Christian culture, which creates Christian politics.

This begs the question, what happened to America's faith?

America was founded as a Christian nation and has been blessed for generations because of it. Over the past two and a half centuries, however, Christians slowly began to pull out of society and retreat into the four walls of the church.

The rise of Dispensational Theology in the late 19th century caused many Christians to begin looking to the sky for a heavenly escape and as a result, abdicate their role in shepherding society.

This is not what our Pilgrim forefathers believed when they sailed from England to America in 1620. Thank God for their vision!

At one time I believed that we were living in the last days of human history and that Jesus was going to return at any moment to rapture His church and judge the world. I grew up in the 70's, when apocalyptic books like *The Late Great Planet Earth* by Hal Lindsey were taking the American church by storm. In addition to hundreds of sermons on the subject, I remember quite vividly the time our church played the *Thief in the Night* film series. In case you don't remember, the series consisted of the following frightening films: *A Thief in the Night*, *A Distant Thunder*, *Image of the Beast*, and *Prodigal Planet*.

The powerful and terrifying concept of an imminent apocalypse defined my view of Christianity well into my married years. And as much as it may have helped me to develop a fear of God, it ultimately left me with many unanswered questions.

Questions like, why did the New Testament writers always refer to the coming of Christ as being near and in their lifetime? And why does the book of Revelation say that the events of the book are "at hand" and will "shortly come to pass?"

I pondered the question, "If the Bible is inspired by God, which it is, why didn't the writers understand that the return of Christ would be 2,000+ years later?"

Furthermore, why would Christ establish a church in the first century that was doomed to deteriorate and fail a mere 20 centuries later? Late nights watching Jack Van Impe and John Hagee, with their elaborate prophetic charts and graphs and no real alternative, kept me locked into a downward spiraling system. The more complicated the story, the more convincing it became.

My apocalyptic house of cards finally collapsed, however, when I watched a video called *Demystifying Revelation* with Gary DeMar, Ken Gentry, and Ralph Barker in the year 2000. I remember the incredible boost of faith I received when I heard them say that the Bible meant exactly what it said when it referred to the timing of Christ's return.

Using history, they showed me how most of the prophetic events of the Bible were fulfilled with stunning accuracy in the years leading up to and including the destruction of Jerusalem in A.D. 70.

I urge you take off your "last days" glasses for just a moment and read the following verses again:

> Matthew 16:27-28 (NIV) For the Son of Man is going to come in his Father's glory with his angels, and then he will reward each person according to what they have done. Truly I tell you, some who are standing here will not taste death before they see the Son of Man coming in his kingdom.

> Matthew 10:23 (NIV) When you are persecuted in one place, flee to another. Truly I tell you, you will not finish going through the towns of Israel before the Son of Man comes.

Matthew 24:29-34 (NIV) Immediately after the distress of those days 'the sun will be darkened, and the moon will not give its light; the stars will fall from the sky, and the heavenly bodies will be shaken.' [Isaiah 13:10; 34:4]

Then will appear the sign of the Son of Man in heaven. And then all the peoples of the earth [the tribes of the land] will mourn when they see the Son of Man coming on the clouds of heaven, with power and great glory. [Daniel 7:13-14]

And he will send his angels with a loud trumpet call, and they will gather his elect from the four winds, from one end of the heavens to the other. Now learn this lesson from the fig tree: As soon as its twigs get tender and its leaves come out, you know that summer is near. Even so, when you see all these things, you know that it [he] is near, right at the door. Truly I tell you, this generation will certainly not pass away until all these things have happened.

Romans 16:20 (NIV) The God of peace will soon crush Satan under your feet. The grace of our Lord Jesus be with you.

Hebrews 10:37 (NIV) For, 'In just a little while, he who is coming will come and will not delay.'

James 5:7-9 (NIV) "Be patient, then, brothers and sisters, until the Lord's coming. See how the farmer waits for the land to yield its valuable crop, patiently waiting for the autumn and spring rains. You too, be patient and stand firm, because the Lord's coming is near. 9 Don't grumble against one another, brothers and sisters, or you will be judged. The Judge is standing at the door!"

1 John 2:18 (NIV) Dear children, this is the last hour; and as you have heard that the antichrist is coming, even now many antichrists have come. This is how we know it is the last hour.

Revelation 1:1 (NIV) The revelation from Jesus Christ, which God gave him to show his servants what must soon take place. He made it known by sending his angel to his servant John,

Revelation 1:3 (NIV) Blessed is the one who reads aloud the words of this prophecy, and blessed are those who hear it and take to heart what is written in it, because the time is near.

Revelation 22:6-7 (NIV) The angel said to me, "These words are trustworthy and true. The Lord, the God who inspires the prophets, sent his angel to show his servants the things that must soon take place." "Look, I am coming soon! Blessed is the one who keeps the words of the prophecy written in this scroll."

Revelation 22:10 (NIV) Then he told me, "Do not seal up the words of the prophecy of this scroll, because the time is near.

If the Bible is the infallible word of God, which it is, can this many passages inaccurately predict the timing of Christ's return? I believe absolutely not.

Let's be honest with the text. Matthew 24:34, for example, requires that the great tribulation occur before the current generation (about 40 years) passed away. Add approximately 40 years to A.D. 33, and you'll find yourself in the midst of one of the most horrific events in history: the crucifixion of millions of Jews, the destruction of the Temple, and the burning of the Holy City of Jerusalem. The entire Old Covenant system collapsed at that time. Not a single sacrifice has been offered by the Jewish people since that time. Most people fail to realize that this was perhaps the most significant event in prophetic history.

I know you're skeptical and have a lot of questions, so I highly encourage you to read *Is Jesus Coming Soon?* and *Last Days Madness* by Gary DeMar, for more information. His ability to interpret the Bible plainly and his clear writing style will captivate you and build your faith.

If the great tribulation was a past event, what about the return of Christ?

In Matthew 24:30, Jesus states:

> "Then will appear the sign of the Son of Man in heaven. And then all the peoples of the earth will mourn when they see the Son of Man coming on the clouds of heaven, with power and great glory"

Most Christians believe this is referring to the Second Coming of Christ. But is it? Jesus is actually quoting directly from Daniel 7:13-14, which reads:

> "In my vision at night I looked, and there before me was one like a son of man, coming with the clouds of heaven. He approached the Ancient of Days and was led into his presence. He was given authority, glory and sovereign power; all nations and peoples of every language worshiped him. His dominion is an everlasting dominion that will not pass away, and his kingdom is one that will never be destroyed."

To me this it is clear that this passage teaches that Jesus is going up in the clouds of heaven and NOT coming down to earth. He is going to God the Father, who will give Him an everlasting Kingdom. This event must have happened before A.D. 70, because Jesus said that the entire Olivet Discourse would be fulfilled before this generation passed away.

It is true that Christ will one day return to earth bodily (1 Thess. 4:16) and defeat his final enemy, which is death (1 Corinthians 15:25-26). Until then, he is reigning in heaven on the throne of His Father David (Acts 2:33-36 and Heb. 1).

If most prophecy has been fulfilled, now what?

Is there anything left to happen on God's prophetic calendar? You bet. The darkest part of human history is over. We now have the hope of a growing and expanding Kingdom already underway!

In the book of Daniel, we are given a vivid picture of the timing, power, and scope of Christ's Kingdom. Daniel 2 tells us about the dream King Nebuchadnezzar had of the great image made of gold, silver, bronze, iron, and clay. Daniel interprets the image as representing four kingdoms that would rule on the earth: Babylon, Medo-Persia, Greece, and Rome. Incidentally, this passage does not teach that there will be a second or "revived" Roman empire in the future.

The stone that crushes the image in verses 34-35 represents Christ's Kingdom. In Daniel 2:44, Daniel states that in the days of the fourth kingdom (Rome), "the God of heaven will set up a kingdom which shall never be destroyed; and the kingdom shall not be left to other people; it shall break in pieces and consume all these kingdoms, and it shall stand forever."

Hundreds of years after Daniel made this remarkable prophecy, John the Baptist arrives on the scene, during the Roman empire, and calls people to, "Repent, for the kingdom of heaven is at hand!" Of course, Jesus also taught that His Kingdom was about to be inaugurated. In Matthew 4:17, Jesus also states, "Repent: for the kingdom of heaven is at hand."

The Kingdom of God is growing, and we've only just begun. In Deuteronomy 7:9, God promises that his love and faithfulness will extend to a thousand generations. And Galatians 3 reminds us that all those who have faith in Christ are heir to the promises of Israel.

If a generation is about 40 years, then we've only completed about 6,000 years of history and have at least 34,000 years to go! We're not living in the last days--we're living in the exciting days of the early church!

Every decision we make today, especially how we train our children, will make an impact for thousands of years to come.

God has given us an opportunity to make a tremendous impact for His Kingdom. This is an exciting time to be alive in history. Don't get caught up in the doom and gloom sensationalism of the liberal media and prophecy writers. Instead, think about your grandchildren's grandchildren. What kind of a vision will you leave them with after your passing?

For more information on the growing Kingdom of Christ, I encourage you to read *Postmillennialism: An Eschatology of Hope* by Keith Matthison.

I am also excited to announce that *Tolle Lege Press* is currently in the process of publishing Ken Gentry's two-volume commentary on the Book of Revelation.

The most appropriate way to end this book is to chant the motto of the Revolutionary War, "No King but King Jesus!"

ABOUT THE AUTHOR
BRANDON VALLORANI

Brandon Vallorani is a serial entrepreneur and accomplished CEO, recognized by peers and media outlets as a visionary leader and powerhouse executive who "knows a thing or two about marketing."

Author of Amazon bestseller, *The Wolves and the Mandolin: Celebrating Life's Privileges In A Harsh World* (ForbesBooks; 2017), Brandon begins with the Vallorani family's modest beginnings in Italy, regales readers with legend-worthy stories of great-grandfather Luigi's first years in America, and culminates with his journey into entrepreneurship.

After graduating from West Virginia University with a Bachelor's Degree of Fine Arts in Graphic Design, Vallorani began his career in the non-profit sector in 1998, and quickly rose through the ranks to Executive Vice President. He simultaneously earned his Master of Business Administration from Thomas More University in 2004.

He went on to work with another non-profit from 2004-2010. In 2004, Brandon also co-founded Tolle Lege Press (TLP) with his father, Ray.

As their first project, TLP raised over $100,000 for the reproduction of a historic masterpiece: *The 1599 Geneva Bible*. The *Geneva Bible* bears much historical significance to the Reformation period, and came to America with the Mayflower, but had been lost in obscurity and available only without modern fonts, spelling, or punctuation. The first updated reproduction was published by TLP in 2006.

Since its publication, TLP has distributed over 140,000 copies of the Geneva Bible in 14 different formats. and published over 20 additional titles through the years.

In 2007, Brandon branched out into yet another entrepreneurial endeavor, with the founding of PatriotDepot.com that would eventually explode into a network of websites and webstores known as Liberty Alliance.

Recognized on the Inc. 5000 list of America's fastest growing privately-held companies for five consecutive years (2012-

2016), Liberty Alliance was acquired by Liftable Media, Inc. in 2017, and Vallorani shifted his focus to marketing products through KeepandBear.com, MAGAfun.com, and RepublicanLegion.com (acquired by Yippy, Inc. in 2019).

After developing a firm, Romulus Marketing, to help others in the Conservative and religious markets build their empires, once again a Vallorani company received a nod for their success when placed on the Inc. 5000 list in 2019.

Also in 2019, Brandon's second book, co-authored with Doug Giles, *Would Jesus Vote for Trump?* was released.

For the next two years, Brandon served as the CEO for DeDonato Enterprises, LLC, before it was acquired by CBMJ, Inc., a publicly traded company where he now serves on the Board of Directors. During that time he also co-founded Southern Stock Transfer Company, LLC, and sold it in 2021.

A Forbes.com contributor, he has been interviewed by numerous podcasts, magazines, and sites.

Holding dual citizenship with Italy, Vallorani resides in Metro-Atlanta with his wife, with whom he shares seven children, and three grandchildren. Today, Brandon is focused on his consulting and publishing business, and assists businesses with branding and marketing.

PHOTO GALLERY

Brandon's grandfather, Eugene Vallorani,
serving in the U.S. Army-Airforce during WWII

Brandon's uncle Gene Vallorani and father Ray Vallorani
working at WBOY News circa

Brandon Vallorani on his property in Georgia

Brandon Vallorani with his father Ray, his sons Adam, Isaac, and Levi and NASCAR Driver, Brennan Poole, with the truck Brandon's company sponsored

Brandon Vallorani with Governor Scott Walker (R-WI)

*Brandon enjoying
NASCAR races with
sons Adam and Isaac*